Celebrating your year

1962

a very special year for

_____

_____

_____

_____

_____

A message from the author:

Welcome to the year 1962.

I trust you will enjoy this fascinating romp down memory lane.

And when you have reached the end of the book, please join me in the battle against AI generated copy-cat books and fake reviews.

Details are at the back of the book.*

Best regards,
Bernard Bradforsand-Tyler.

Contents

1962 Family Life in the USA	8
Life in the United Kingdom	15
Our Love Affair with Cars	19
Tuning in to Television	24
Most Popular TV Shows of 1962	25
Cold War–Nuclear Weapons Testing	29
Cuban Missile Crisis	30
Cold War–Space Race	31
Cold War–Battlefield Vietnam	32
Mississippi Riots at Ole Miss	35
Nelson Mandela Arrested	36
Indo-Sino War Escalates	37
1962 in Cinema and Film	40
Top Grossing Films of the Year	41
A Decade of Cinema Epics	42
Influential Cult Classics in Film	45
Marilyn Monroe Life and Death	46
The Pop Art of Andy Warhol	47
Who Were The Rat Pack?	50
Musical Memories	51
1962 Billboard Top 30 Songs	52
Fashion Trends of the 1960s	55
Katherine Johnson NASA's Computer	64
Science and Medicine	65
Also in Sports	67
Other News from 1962	68
Famous People Born in 1962	72
1962 in Numbers	76
Image Attributions	84

Advertisement

How to take a call without missing a mouthful

It's easy when you have a kitchen extension phone. You can feed the baby... check the grocery list... fix a formula or seven-minute frosting... and keep right at it when the telephone rings.

A kitchen extension saves you time and steps every day, lets you take and make calls when you're busiest.

Extension phones for happier living—where your family works, plays and sleeps—cost little for the convenience they give. Your choice of styles and colors. To order, just call the Business Office or ask your telephone man.

 BELL TELEPHONE SYSTEM

How to take a call without missing a mouthful

It's easy when you have a kitchen extension phone. You can feed the baby... check the grocery list... fix a formula or seven-minute frosting... and keep right at it when the telephone rings.

A kitchen extension saves you time and steps every day, lets you take and make calls when you're busiest.

Extension phones for happier living—where your family works, plays and sleeps—cost little for the convenience they give. Your choice of styles and colors. To order, just call the Business Office or ask your telephone man.

Bell Telephone System

Let's flashback to 1962, a very special year.

Was this the year you were born?

Was this the year you were married?

Whatever the reason, this book is a celebration of your year,

THE YEAR 1962.

Turn the pages to discover a book packed with fun-filled fabulous facts. We look at the people, the places, the politics and the pleasures that made 1962 unique and helped shape the world we know today.

So get your time-travel suit on, and enjoy this trip down memory lane, to rediscover what life was like, back in the year 1962.

1962 Family Life in the USA

Imagine if time-travel was a reality, and one fine morning you wake up to find yourself flashed back in time, back to the year 1962.

What would life be like for a typical family, in a typical town, somewhere in America?

A stylish modern suburban family kitchen in 1962.

The year 1962 brought us closer than we had ever been to the brink of a third world war. It was a year of political and social tensions. Yet we often reminisce about this period as a time of prosperity, when babies were born in record numbers, fathers had jobs for life, and our standard of living surpassed that which our parents only dreamt of.

In 1962, after two years of recession, the economy bounced back. A culture of consume and discard flourished, driven by an advertising industry which instilled in us the belief that we constantly needed more and more, bigger and better. Americans consumed a whopping one-third of the world's goods and services.[1]

[1] exploros.com/summary/Economy-in-the-1950s.

The start of the decade marked a high point for the Baby Boomer generation (1946-1964). Children under nineteen represented 38% of our nation,[1] a percentage which has been in decline ever since.

The single income family was still the norm, with fathers commuting to work while mothers were encouraged to stay at home.

Cooking time together for a family in the early '60s.

One-third of us lived in the suburbs, having fled the decaying cities for the dream of a house on our own land, a car, a dog and 2.3 kids. 80% of households owned an automobile. The 40-hour workweek with paid leave had become the norm and we spent more on leisure activities, health care and education than ever before.

[1] census.gov/library/publications/1963/compendia/statab/84ed.html, page 6.

Advertisement

Only Frigidaire Ranges have the Pull 'N Clean Oven!
slides out for easy cleaning—glides back for carefree cooking

Silver Anniversary of Frigidaire Ranges! The giant charm bracelet symbolizes the twenty-fifth year since the first Frigidaire Electric Range was created for American homemakers. Celebrate with us! See the beautiful Frigidaire Flair (looks built-in, but isn't) at your dealer's now.

First outstanding feature you'll notice on this new 1962 Silver Anniversary Frigidaire Range is the Pull 'N Clean Oven. You can clean it standing up—easier and faster than any other oven!

This model also gives you the exclusive Broiler Control that turns out roasts, steaks and chops done just the way you want them. For example, on steaks you dial your choice of rare, medium or well-done. Exclusive design of the Spatter-Free Broiler Pan makes for easy clean-ups, too.

The unwatched pot *does* boil—but it won't burn on the Frigidaire Heat Minder. Just set it and forget it! Automatically minds the bacon or simmers the stew and guards against boiling over or scorching. On all Imperial Ranges and Custom Imperial Ranges, Flair and Built-In Cooking Tops.

See your dealer now for the full story about the 1962 Silver Anniversary Frigidaire Ranges, products of General Motors.

Send 25¢ for colorful new 24-page booklet, "Frigidaire Kitchen Ideas." P.O. Box 124, Dept. 38, Dayton 1, Ohio.

Only Frigidaire Ranges have a Pull 'N Clean Oven!
slides out for easy cleaning—glides back for carefree cooking

First outstanding feature you'll notice on this new 1962 Silver Anniversary Frigidaire Range is the Pull 'N Clean Oven. You can clean it standing up—easier and faster than any other oven!

This model also gives you the exclusive Broiler Control that turns out roasts, steaks and chops done just the way you want them. For example, on steaks you dial your choice of rare, medium or well-done. Exclusive design of the Splatter-Free Broiler Pan makes for easy clean-ups, too.

The unwatched pot *does* boil—but it won't burn on the Frigidaire Heat Minder. Just set it and forget it! Automatically minds the bacon or simmers the stew and guards against boiling over or scorching. On all Imperial Ranges and Custom Imperial Ranges, Flair and Built-In Cooking Tops.

See your dealer now for the full story about the 1962 Silver Anniversary Frigidaire Ranges, products of General Motors.

Advertisement

What does it take to feel like a man?

In today's world... What does it take to feel like a man?

It takes *action* to feel like a man. Takes *pride,* too, and good, skillful *training.* Join the modern Army's Combat Arms program and you'll have all three.

Pride? In Combat Arms it makes no difference whether you select Infantry, Armor, or Artillery. You'll be proud of any one of them. And you'll end up proud of yourself, too.

Action? In today's modern Army it's *go* all the way. Every unit is smooth, fast, and flexible. And every day brings fresh, new challenges. It takes real men to cope with them.

Training? In today's world nothing but skilled hands and minds will do. They whole Army is like a huge, well-oiled engine–with men and machines closely interlocked. It takes *men* to fit into this kind of picture.

And of course you have other choices, too. Want Combat Support or Technical Training? Then ask for Electronics, Heavy Equipment, Transportation or Maintenance. It's as simple as that. If you're *qualified,* your choice is *guaranteed before you enlist.* Find out how to feel like a man in today's fast-changing world. See your local Army recruiter today!

For women, marriage and children were still the priority. Most women aged 30-34 were married (88%) and the majority (90%) had children.[1]

Working women could expect to be paid almost 40% less than their male counterparts. It was universally accepted that a man was the breadwinner of the family, and that a wife should earn less.

Mother with daughters cooking in the early '60s.

The median family income was $6,000 a year.[2] Unemployment stood at 5.5%, with GDP growth at 6.1%.[3]

Average costs in 1962 [4]	
New house	$19.580
New car	$3,125
Washing machine	$190
Vacuum cleaner	$40
A gallon of gasoline	$0.31

[1] From the US Census Bureau-1960 Census: Population, Supplementary Reports: Marital Status of the Population.
[2] census.gov/library/publications/1963/demo/p60-040.html.
[3] thebalance.com/unemployment-rate-by-year-3305506.
[4] thepeoplehistory.com and mclib.info/reference/local-history-genealogy/historic-prices/.

But beyond the glamour and excesses of our pristine, appliance-filled suburban lives, there was another America. One where struggles with poverty, health care, education, housing, racial and sexual inequality, and even the right to vote were brewing the demand for change.

African Americans, women, and other minorities were amplifying their voices. We took to the streets in record numbers—demanding to be heard, demanding change for a better, more egalitarian America. The 1960s would become the decade of reform and revolution.

American civil rights protests in the early '60s.

In 1962, the US Supreme court disallowed race separation on public transportation; Martin Luther King Jr. was arrested for protest activities and sentenced to jail; John F. Kennedy served his only full year as President— he would be assassinated the following year.

Adding to the unrest, Cold War politics dominated our lives as the Nuclear Arms Race and the Space Race were in full swing. 1962 brought us to the brink of nuclear war. While we stockpiled nuclear weapons at a frenzied pace, nuclear bomb testing also peaked. Meanwhile, space exploration turned outer-space into the next Cold War battleground. We would endure another three decades of tensions between the two superpowers before the Cold War finally ended with the dissolution of the Soviet Union in 1991.

Advertisement

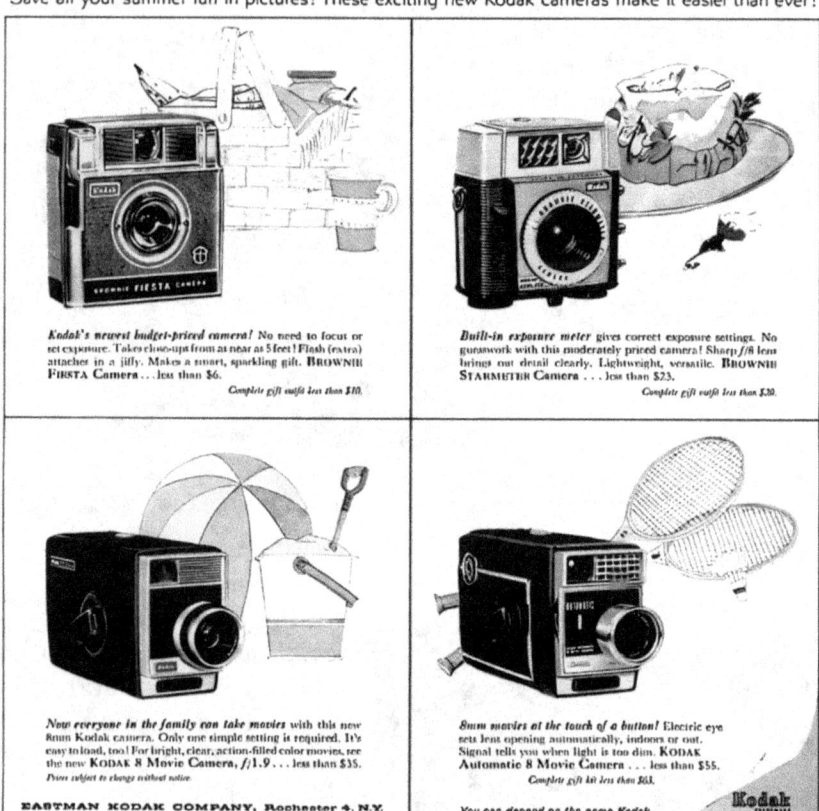

Fun-savers for '62... from Kodak!

Save all your summer fun in picture! These exciting new Kodak cameras make it easier than ever!

Kodak's newest budget-priced camera! No need to focus or set exposure. Takes close-ups from as near as 5 feet! Flash (extra) attaches in a jiffy. Makes a smart, sparkling gift. Brownie Fiesta Camera... less than $6. *Complete gift outfit less than $10*

Built-in exposure meter gives correct exposure settings. No guesswork with this moderately priced camera! Shap $f/8$ lens brings out detail clearly. Lightweight, versatile. Brownie Starmeter Camera... less than $23. *Complete gift outfit less than $29.*

Now everyone in the family can take movies with this new 8mm Kodak camera. Only one simple setting is required. It's easy to load, too! For bright, clear, action-filled color movies, see the new Kodak 8 Movie Camera, $f/1.9$... less than $35.

8mm movies at the touch of a button! Electric eye sets lens opening automatically, indoors or out. Signal tells you when light is too dim. Kodak Automatic 8 Movie Camera... less than $55. *Complete gift outfit less than $63.*

You can <u>depend</u> on the name Kodak.

Life in the United Kingdom

Now just imagine you flashed back to a town in 1962 England or Western Europe.

Unlike their lavish, consumer-driven counterparts in America, a very different picture would await you.

By 1962, the United Kingdom was still struggling to regain its place on the world stage. It was no longer a superpower, having lost that title, along with many of its former colonies, in the aftermath of the second world war. Rebuilding from the ruins of war had exacted a heavy economic toll on the country. Yet beneath the subdued austerity and stoicism, the country was poised for a resurgence of youthful vitality and dynamism, unlike anything it had known before.

London "Bobby" helping kids cross the street.

Artists, writers, academics and musicians were developing their own uniquely British creations. A more expressive, tolerant and open-minded view of the world was being born. It would filter through the streets of London and within a few years the cultural revolution known as the "Swinging Sixties" would, through music, fashion and the arts, place Britain once again at the center of the world.

In the years leading up to 1962 the UK, like much of the western world, enjoyed low unemployment (around 2%), real wage increases, and consumer spending growth. There was spare money for luxuries and leisure pursuits. Prime Minister Harold MacMillan famously summed it up when he stated, "you've never had it so good".[1]

Piccadilly Circus in the early '60s.

MacMillan's conservative voters, however, were not pleased with his economic policies. Feeling the need to invigorate the party, the PM enacted a Cabinet reshuffle. Known as the "Night of the Long Knives", MacMillan dismissed one-third of his aging Cabinet Members in one night, replacing them with younger, more energetic members.

The UK's apparent prosperity masked the relative decline of British competitiveness on the world stage. The UK had slipped far behind its European neighbors and did not come close to the lavish consumerism of the USA.

[1] nationalarchives.gov.uk/education/resources/fifties-britain/youve-never-good/.

By 1962, private car ownership was still rare, and most households continued to rely on public transport. In fact, steam trains continued to run until the mid-'60s. Road networks and telecommunications remained woefully inadequate.

90% of British power was supplied by coal, with inner city power stations, factories and domestic fireplaces belching out sulfur-laden smoke. In December, London suffered a deadly toxic smog killing up to 700 people. The smog was followed by ten weeks of blizzards, ice, and freezing temperatures. "The Big Freeze" brought the UK to a standstill.

Lady on a double-decker bus, early '60s.

Post war Britain had borrowed heavily from USA and Canada in order to survive and rebuild. Yet Britain failed to modernize its industries in the same way France, Germany, and other war-torn countries had succeeded in doing.

In 1962, The Beatles released their first album; The Rolling Stones made their debut at London's Marquee Club; the first James Bond film was released; and Anthony Burgess published *A Clockwork Orange*.

It would not be long before British artists would shake the world. British youth would lead the cultural revolution of the '60s and London would be their epicenter.

The Beatles with Ed Sullivan. From left Ringo Starr, George Harrison, Ed Sullivan, John Lennon, and Paul McCartney, 9th February 1964.

Advertisement

Chrysler New Yorker!
You may well ask why it doesn't cost more

This is particularly true if you've done some comparison shopping in the New Yorker price bracket.

And if you haven't, we encourage you to do so.

We believe you'll make the revealing discovery that Chrysler's finest gives you so much more of the kind of luxury you deserve.

New Yorker's solid Unibody shields you in quiet, full-sized comfort. Sofa-size seats are lavishly cushioned in foam rubber. The driver's seat back is three inches higher for an uncommonly restful riding posture. Deep-pile carpeting runs from door to door.

New Yorker appointments are tastefully impressive without being ostentatious. A husky 340-horsepower engine endows this Chrysler with a dash that belies its dignity.

Explore the field. You'll conclude that luxury has never been so practical as it is in the Chrysler New Yorker.

Three great Chryslers... Newport · 300 · New Yorker...
Again, no Jr. editions to jeopardize your investment!

Our Love Affair with Cars

By 1962, 65.8 million cars were on our roads. And with more and more cars purchased each year, owning a car was no longer considered a luxury reserved only for the wealthy.

Artists image of the 1962 Pontiac Grand Prix.

Increased car ownership and the creation of the National Highway System gave us a new sense of freedom. Office commuters could live further out from city centers and commute quickly and comfortably to work. The suburbanization of America, which began in the early '50s, now saw one-third of Americans living in the suburbs. Furthermore, rural areas were no longer isolated, benefiting from access to food, medical and other supplies.

Services related businesses such as drive-through or drive-in restaurants and drive-in cinemas were commonplace and popular, especially among the younger generation.

[1] fhwa.dot.gov/ohim/summary95/mv200.pdf.

An astonishing one in six working adults were employed directly or indirectly by the American automobile industry.

1962 Chevrolet Chevy Impala 4-door sports sedan.

Detroit was America's car manufacturing powerhouse, where "the Big Three" (Ford, General Motors and Chrysler) produced year-on-year bigger, longer, and heavier gas-guzzlers to satisfy the midcentury consumer desire for style over efficiency and safety. Decorative chrome and tail fins reached new heights towards the end of the '50s. However, by the early '60s, the consumer mentality began turning against this extravagance and excess.

Led in part by the success of the imported Volkswagen Beetle and the economic recession of 1958, consumer demand began shifting towards smaller, more compact, cheaper and safer vehicles.

The scene was set for Japanese small car manufacturers to take on the Big Three.

Four car-producing countries dominated in 1962: England, France, and Germany, with America in the top spot. However, this elite group would soon be rocked by the aggressive expansion of the Japanese automotive industry. Within 5 years, Japan would rise to become the second largest car producing country, behind only the US.

1962 European car advertisements for Fiat 1100 (top left), Volkswagen (right), and Renault R4 (below).

Car ownership in other countries lagged behind the USA, even with the rising incomes and living standards of most western nations. Public transport was still the norm for European and British commuters.

In Asia, the car had yet to become mainstream. Less than 1% of the population in China and India could afford a car.

Advertisement

New measure of fashion... new concept of reliability!

Quality you will recognize in every stylish feature! Reliability you will appreciate at every effortless turn of the wheel! Never have they so aptly demonstrated Olds superiority as they do in the magnificent new

Ninety-Eight Oldsmobile

There's smooth powerful V-8 action in every Olds.
Ninety-Eight. Super 88. Dynamic 88. F-85. Starfire.

Advertisement

When you first drive up in a Cadillac,

even old friends see you in a new light. This is going to be especially true when you make your initial entrance in a 1963 Cadillac. A newly refined engine moves the big car so silently you must announce your arrival with a tap of the horn. And when the inevitable inspection comes, be prepared for "Ohs" and "Ahs" at the elegance of the widest choice of personal options in Cadillac history. Is there someone you'd like to surprise? Go ahead and do it. Your Cadillac dealer will help you stage the scene.

Tuning in to Television

Television ownership in America soared during the '50s and early '60s, increasing sharply from only 9% of households in 1950, to 90% by 1962. During the '50s, television's "Golden Age", most of the programs were broadcast live from New York in the ongoing tradition of old-time radio broadcasting. But by the '60s, made-for-TV programs coming out of Los Angeles dominated our screens.

By 1962, the three national US television networks were able to reach the most remote parts of the country, bringing a shared common experience to both urban and rural America. Television had quickly become our preferred source of entertainment and information.

TV time in the early '60s.

Elsewhere in the world, access to television was not nearly as widespread as in the US. Due to the extreme costs of setting up networks and financing programs, many countries did not begin television broadcasts until the mid-'60s or later.

In many countries, television networks were government owned or subsidized. This allowed for more focus on serious documentaries and news broadcasts, without the constant concern of generating advertising revenue.

Most Popular TV Shows of 1962

1	The Beverly Hillbillies	11	Dr. Kildare
2	Candid Camera	=	The Jack Benny Show
=	The Red Skelton Show	13	What's My Line?
4	Bonanza	14	The Ed Sullivan Show
=	The Lucy Show	15	Hazel
6	The Andy Griffith Show	16	I've Got a Secret
7	Ben Casey	17	The Jackie Gleason Show
=	The Danny Thomas Show	18	The Defenders
9	The Dick Van Dyke Show	19	The Garry Moore Show
10	Gunsmoke	=	To Tell the Truth
		=	Lassie

* From the Nielsen Media Research 1962-'63 season of top-rated primetime TV series in the USA.

In 1962, the dominance of dramatic Westerns gave way to the frivolity of variety programs, game shows and sitcoms. Five of the top 10 programs for the year were situation comedies, following the format of 1950s sitcom sensation *I Love Lucy*.

The Lucy Show was Lucille Ball's follow-up to *I Love Lucy*, securing her two Emmy Awards during its six-year run.

Mary Tyler Moore & Dick Van Dyke in
The Dick Van Dyke Show (CBS. 1961-1966).

Lucille Ball and Vivian Vance in
The Lucy Show (CBS. 1962-1968).

CBS sitcom *The Dick Van Dyke Show* ran for five seasons, turning Dick Van Dyke and Mary Tyler Moore into household names.

Both *The Lucy Show* and *The Dick Van Dyke Show* were filmed by Desilu Studios (Lucille Ball and Desi Arnaz) using their 3-camera multiple angle technique. The two shows were the only sitcoms of the time to be filmed in front of live studio audiences.

Advertisement

Check this Sylvania Suburbanite 19" TV against any other 19" TV on these important points and you, too, will rate it #1:

Picture Quality. Only Sylvania of all leading brands of 19" TV sets has a horizontal linearity control that tunes out distortions. Squares always look square–circles, circular–people on screen always keep right proportions.

▫Bonded Tube Protection. Only 19" set with shatterproof safety glass bonded right to the picture tube. No dust can ever filter in to dim your picture. In addition, annoying reflections are reduced 66%. ▫Performance. Automatic gain control makes it unnecessary to readjust contrast and brightness when changing to stations of different signal strength. Good contrast-brightness ratio and high-quality interference rejection assure top performance. ▫Top Mounted Speaker. Front projected for best combination of sound quality and compact size... only $18^7/_8$ wide; $12^3/_8$" deep. Fits where others won't, yet no portable gives you a bigger picture. ▫Much lighter. Weighs only 39 pounds–over 20% lighter than average of other leading 19-inchers.

See why Sylvania 19" TV is rated #1. Check out all its top-rated features for yourself. Make your own comparison at your TV dealer's today!

James Drury in *The Virginian* (CBS. 1962-1968).

Andy Williams as host of *The Andy Williams Show* (NBC. 1962-1971).

The television networks were quick to turn out new programs to keep us tuning in. Here are just a few of the new programs that aired for the first time in 1962: *The Beverly Hillbillies, The Lucy Show, The Virginian, The Andy Williams Show, McHale's Navy,* and *The Tonight Show* starring Johnny Carson (1962-'92).

Ernest Borngine in *McHale's Navy* (Revue 1962-'63, Universal 1963-'66).

The Tonight Show debut, host Johnny Carson with (L) Skitch Henderson and (R) Ed McMahon (NBC. 1962-'72).

Advertisement

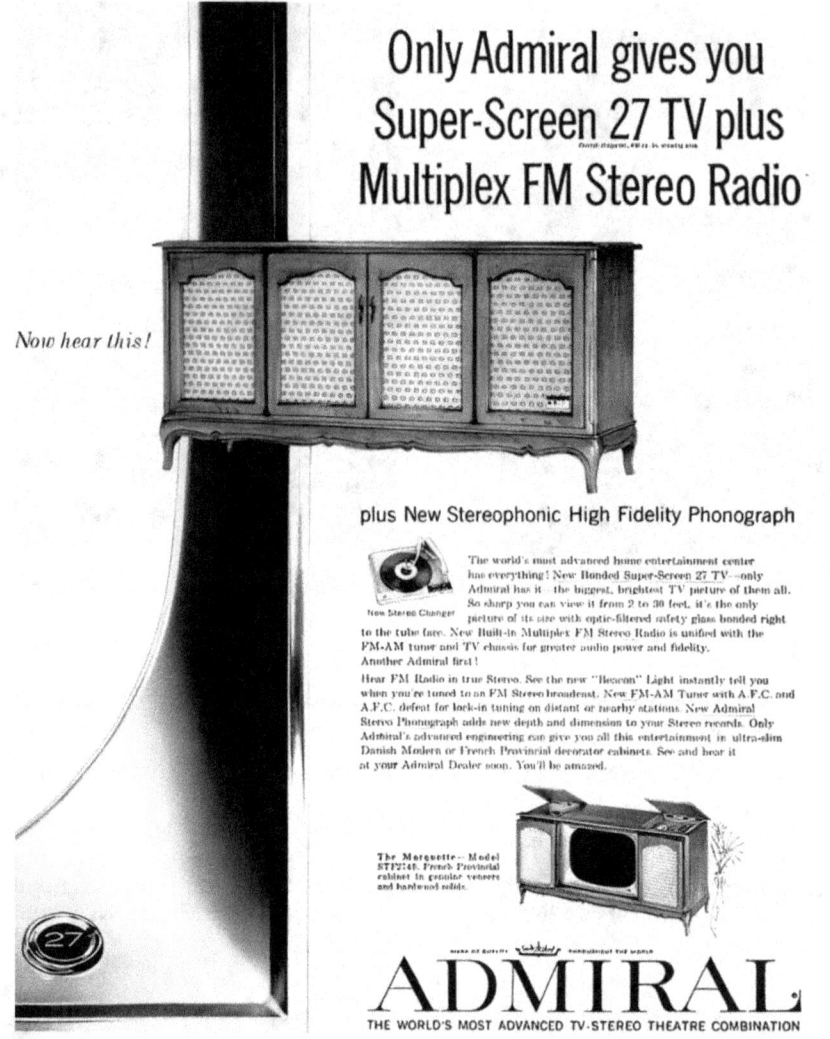

Only Admiral gives you Super-Screen 27 TV plus Multiplex FM Stereo Radio
Plus new Stereophonic High Fidelity Phonograph.

The world's most advanced home entertainment center has everything! New Bonded Super-Screen 27 TV–only Admiral has it–the biggest, brightest TV picture of them all. So sharp you can view it from 2 to 30 feet. It's the only picture of its size with optic-filtered safety glass bonded right to the tube face. New Built-in Multiplex FM Stereo Radio is unified with the FM-AM tuner and TV chassis for greater audio power and fidelity. Another Admiral first!

Hear FM Radio in true Stereo. See the new "Beacon" Light instantly tell you when you're tuned to an FM Stereo broadcast. New FM-AM Tuner with A.F.C. and A.P.C. defeat for lock-in tuning on distant or nearby stations. New Admiral Stereo Phonograph adds new depth and dimension to your Stereo records. Only Admiral's advanced engineering can give you all this entertainment in ultra-slim Danish Modern or French Provincial decorator cabinets. See and hear it at your Admiral Dealer soon. You'll be amazed.

Cold War-Nuclear Weapons Testing

Cold War tensions between the two former allies—the USSR and the USA—continued from post war 1945 until 1991. Starting in the USA as policies for communist containment, the mutual misunderstanding and distrust escalated from political squabbling to a military Nuclear Arms Race, giving the two superpowers the pretext needed to stockpile and test nuclear bombs on a massive scale.

After the Soviets abruptly ended the 1958 moratorium on nuclear testing, 1962 saw an astonishing 175 nuclear bomb tests carried out by the two superpowers, more than double the annual Cold War average.[1]

Operation Dominic Swordfish, Pacific Ocean, 11th May 1952.

The Soviets conducted 79 tests, including 4 of the top 6 biggest bombs of all time. Most were atmospheric free-fall detonations. Of particular interest, as proof of battlefield capability, were an air launch test deployed from a cruise missile, and another deployed from a rocket.

Operation Storax Sedan, Nevada, 6th July 1952.

The US responded with a series of 96 nuclear tests, including the first and only space test. On 9th July, the rocket-launched *Starfish Prime* detonated at an altitude of 400 km (250 mi), causing an electromagnetic pulse and aura visible across the Pacific Ocean. The intense radiation belt damaged $1/3$ of the satellites in low earth orbit.

By 1962, the USA had stockpiled 25,540 nuclear weapons, against the Soviet's 3,322 weapons. The UK was the only other nation in this elite group, with 288 weapons.[2]

[1] armscontrol.org/factsheets/nucleartesttally.
[2] tandfonline.com/doi/pdf/10.2968/066004008.

Cuban Missile Crisis   16th–28th October 1962

By 1962, the USA's vastly superior stash of nuclear arsenals was a grave concern to the Soviets. Even more so were America's nuclear missile bases in Italy and Turkey, with Moscow within easy reach. To address this imbalance, Soviet leader Nikita Khrushchev began shipping nuclear armed ballistic missiles to Cuba.

Determined to prevent this buildup of weapons on America's doorstep, President John F. Kennedy placed a naval quarantine (blockade) around Cuba, demanding the Soviets unilaterally withdraw and dismantle their bases. It was an illegal and risky move.

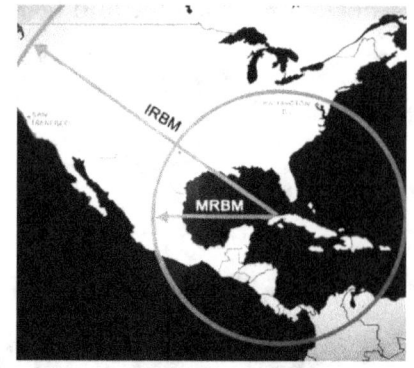

Potential reach of Soviet medium-range (MRBM) and intermediate-range ballistic missiles (IRBM), if launched from Cuba.

For 13 days in October 1962, the world braced itself for nuclear war. Soviet ships circled the Cuban blockade, as the leaders of the two Superpowers sought a mutually acceptable end to the standoff.

On 28th October, Khrushchev and Kennedy reached a deal—the Soviets would dismantle their bases and remove their missiles from Cuba. Kennedy publicly guaranteed the US would not invade Cuba. It appeared that Khrushchev had capitulated to Kennedy's demands. In private, Kennedy had agreed to withdraw the US nuclear arsenals from Turkey and Italy, insisting this part of the deal be kept a secret.

Many decades later, declassified documents would show just how close we came to a global nuclear war, and how determined Kennedy was to retain his strong-man public image.

President Kennedy signing the Cuba Quarantine Proclamation. White House, 23rd Oct 1962.

In the aftermath of the crisis, a Moscow-Washington hotline was established to provide the superpower leaders direct lines of communication, if needed for de-escalation of any future tensions.

Cold War–Space Race

Throughout the 1960s, the Cold War dominated our lives on the ground and in the skies. Cold War tensions affected everything from our politics and education, to our interests in fashion and popular culture. By 1962, the USSR had achieved many firsts in the Space Race, putting them at a military, technological and intellectual advantage.

Cosmonaut Yuri Gagarin.

Yuri Gagarin became the first human in space, circling the earth once in a 108-minute orbital flight on 12th Apr 1961. The Russian's success came as a huge blow to the Americans, who had hoped to be the first to send a man to space.

After repeated technical delays, astronaut Alan Shepard had the bitter-sweet honor of being the second man (first American) in space on 5th May 1961. NASA's vastly inferior Mercury-Redstone 3 brought him for a short, 15-minute suborbital trajectory before falling back to earth.

Astronaut John H. Glenn Jr., wearing a Mercury pressure suit, Feb 1962.

NASA's first full orbit of earth with a man on board occurred on 20th Feb 1962, nearly a full year behind the Soviets. Astronaut John Glenn made three full orbits of the Earth.

A second, almost identical mission carrying astronaut Scott Carpenter was launched on 24th May, with a third longer (6-orbit) mission carrying astronaut Walter Schirra on 3rd Oct.

Throughout the decade the USSR continued to lead the Space Race with longer space flights, more complex space walks and challenging technical activities performed while in orbit.

Ultimately the USA would achieve its goal, winning the Space Race in 1969 when Neil Armstrong and Edwin "Buzz" Aldrin landed, planted the American flag, and walked on the moon for 2 hours 15 minutes.

Cold War–Battlefield Vietnam

Fearful that a "domino effect" would see an uncontained spread of communism across the world, the US committed to supporting South Vietnam, financially and militarily, during its 30-year-long bloody civil war against North Vietnam (the Viet Cong). At the same time, communist China and USSR were jointly aiding the Viet Cong's invasion southward. Vietnam had become a Cold War battlefield.

Under the leadership of President Kennedy, America's involvement in the Vietnam War (known in Vietnam as the American War) was officially limited to training South Vietnamese soldiers in combat methods. However, US Forces did engage in secret attacks against the Viet Cong, with the President's authorization.

US Green Beret conducting training, 1961.

In January 1962, US aircraft began spraying lethal herbicides to defoliate the dense jungle vegetation where the Viet Cong were suspected of hiding. Known as *Operation Ranch Hand,* an estimated 400,000 people were killed or maimed due to herbicide exposure.

By years end, the US had sent 11,000 advisers, 300 aircraft, 120 helicopters, plus heavy machinery. America's active military involvement was kept top-secret.

President Kennedy continued to refuse the deployment of US combat troops in Vietnam. However, under the leadership of President Johnson in 1963, US combat troops began arriving by the thousands.

In all, 2.7 million American soldiers served in Vietnam over the ten years to 1973. More than 58,000 Americans died in battle, in addition to the more than 3 million Vietnamese (civilians and soldiers from both sides of battle).[1]

[1] britannica.com/event/Vietnam-War.

Advertisement

a matchless new expression of a famous tradition:
The New Royal for '62...

With all the virtues that made Royal Manuals famous–low cost, hard work, long life, high trade-in and a pleasant way with secretaries. Your nearby Royal McBee representative wants you to see the new Royal '62 in action. Before you buy a typewriter, let him show you why Royal typewriters–manual and electric–are your best buy.

Advertisement

Trust Swanson for fried chicken that's meaty and tender

Swanson TV Brand Fried Chicken Dinner

Tasty proof that Swanson knows the secret of frying chicken that's crisp outside—juicy and tender inside. This Swanson TV Brand Dinner uses only the choicest pieces—breasts, thighs or drumsticks, wings—never a piece of backbone. Served with fluffy whipped potatoes and garden-good mixed vegetables. This is the kind of eating everybody in the family loves.

12 DELICIOUS TV DINNERS TO CHOOSE FROM

Trust Swanson for the best in frozen dinners

Trust Swanson for fried chicken that's meaty and tender.

Tasty proof that Swanson knows the secret of frying chicken that's crisp outside–juicy and tender inside. This Swanson TV Brand Dinner uses only the choicest pieces–breasts, thighs or drumsticks, wings–never a piece of backbone. Served with fluffy whipped potatoes and garden-good mixed vegetables. This is the kind of eating everybody in the family loves.

12 delicious TV dinners to choose from.

Trust Swanson for the best in frozen dinners.

Mississippi Riots at Ole Miss — 30th September 1962

Violence erupted in Oxford, Mississippi, over the registration of Air Force veteran James Meredith to the University of Mississippi (Ole Miss) to study Political Science. His earlier acceptance had been withdrawn when the registrar discovered he was African-American. Ordered by Federal Court to admit Meredith, Mississippi Governor Ross Barret personally blocked Meredith from entering the campus. On 28th Sept, Governor Barret was found guilty of civil contempt.

Two days later, on the eve of Meredith's registration, soldiers, police, and federal marshals surrounded Ole Miss as a mob of 2,500 arrived to block Meredith's entry. Riots quickly broke out, continuing throughout the night. The mob attacked with acid-filled bottles, Molotov cocktails, guns, bricks, and bulldozers.

James Meredith walking to class accompanied by US federal marshals, 1st Oct 1962.

By 6am, a further 25,000 soldiers arrived. The violence lasted 15 hours. 300 rioters were arrested. More than 200 federal agents and soldiers were wounded. Two civilians had been murdered.

US Army trucks with federal agents roll across the campus on 3rd Oct 1962.

Meredith began classes on 1st Oct with around-the-clock protection. He was shunned by other students and endured constant racial harassment.

Persisting through the intimidation, Meredith graduated in Aug 1963, (having completed two years at Jackson State University in 1960-'61). His enrolment to Ole Miss is regarded as a pivotal moment in the US Civil Rights Movement. In 2016, the University erected his statue on its campus, to acknowledge his ground-breaking achievement.

Nelson Mandela Arrested 5th August 1962

President Nelson Mandela, Oct 1994.

During the 1940s and '50s, South African lawyer and anti-Apartheid activist Nelson Mandela rose through the ranks of the African National Congress (ANC). With the aim of ending the ruling National Party's system of Apartheid, white supremacy and racial segregation, Mandela co-founded and led the new military arm of the ANC– uMkhonto we Sizwe (MK). The Nationals immediately outlawed the ANC and MK.

Mandela had become known as "the Black Pimpernel" for his ability to evade police. He spent months traveling across South Africa disguised as a chauffeur, organizing anti-government activities. On 5th August 1962, outside Durban, Mandela was finally captured.

Two months later he was tried and found guilty of inciting workers to strike and leaving the country without permission. He was sentenced to five years in prison.

Mandela casting his vote in the 1994 elections. It was the first time Mandela had voted in his life.

In October 1963, a new trial began against leaders of the ANC, MK and South Africa's Communist Party, who had been rounded-up together with incriminating documents of their anti-Apartheid activities. All were given life sentences, including Mandela who was still behind bars at the time. Most would serve decades as political prisoners. Mandela was released in 1990, after 27 years in detention.

Nelson Mandela would become the first black President of South Africa in 1994, following the country's first fully democratic election.

Indo-Sino War Escalates 20th Oct – 21st Nov 1962

Military tensions along disputed sections of the border between India and China had been intensifying for many years. While India firmly believed China would never attack, they were inadequately prepared when China's People's Liberation Army (PLA) invaded across multiple sections of border in a simultaneous coordinated assault on 20th Oct 1962. India's PM, Defense Minister, Military Chief of General Staff and Director of Military Operations were all out of the country at the time. India's western allies were preoccupied with the Cuban Missile Crisis.

Above: A standoff at the disputed border between Chinese and Indian soldiers.
Below: Indian troops in battle.
Bottom: Indian soldiers surrender to Chinese forces.

After four days of fierce battles, the PLA secured a substantial portion of the disputed territory. Their 80,000 strong army easily overwhelmed India's 10,000-20,000 force. The PLA had maps, superior weapons, and supplies for the rugged, high-altitude, harsh winter conditions, all of which the Indian troops lacked.

As Indian troops retreated to safe ground, PLA advancement ceased, while leaders on both sides attempted (and failed) to negotiate a settlement.

Heavy fighting continued following the ceasefire, with Chinese forces pushing further into Indian controlled regions. On 19th November, China declared a unilateral ceasefire. China had reclaimed 37,500 sq km (14,500 sq miles) of territory from India, reaching the lines of control it had previously held in 1959. China did not progress any further, marking the war's end.

Advertisement

Meet the team that saves you time

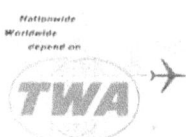

Meet the team that saves you time

You fly to save time. Getting you there on time is a team operation at TWA. Skilled, seasoned flight and ground crews make on-timemanship a habit–to 70 U.S. cities *and* 15 overseas centers. Only TWA flies the StarStream, newest of the transcontinental jets. Four mightly DynaFan engines give the Starstream quicker take-off, swifter climb rate than any other coast-to-coast jet. The StarStream cruises at more than ten miles a minute, and has the tremendous power reserve so vital to maintaining precise flight schedules. On the ground, TWA saves you time with innovations like spilt-second electronic flight information, speeded-up check-in facilities, unique "carousel" baggage delivery. Compare what all airlines offer. Compare... and you'll fly TWA.

Advertisement

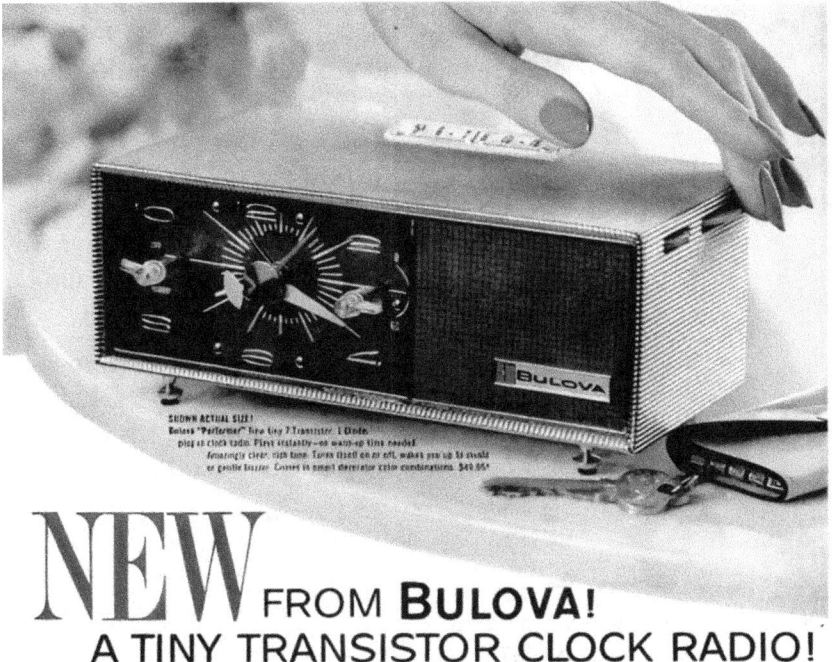

NEW FROM **BULOVA**!
A TINY TRANSISTOR CLOCK RADIO!
So tiny—it fits your smallest bedside table.
So powerful—it fills your largest room with sound.

New from Bulova! A tiny transistor clock radio!
So tiny—it fits your smallest bedside table. So powerful—it fills your largest room with sound.

Bulova "Scout" Magnificent jewelry styling in a new 6-Transistor, 1-Diode pocket portable. Advanced directional antenna pulls in distant stations. Heavy-duty speaker for bell-clear tone. Only $4^1/_4$ inches high. Leather carrying case, earphone. Red, ebony, ivory, blue. $24.95.

Bulova "Conquest" New 7-Transistor, 2-Diode, pocket portable. Has standard AM band for domestic reception–short-wave band for foreign, aviation and ham broadcasts. Complete with leather carrying case, earphone, telescoping antenna. Ebony-ivory, red-ivory, blue-grey. $49.95.

Only Bulova Radios give you handsome jewelry styling for that luxurious look–"matched transistors" of computer quality–extra powerful speakers for room-filling volume–Lock-a-Matic tuning for drift-free, distortion-free reception–Plus one full year guarantee!

See and hear the magnificent Bulova transistor radios and stereo hi-fi portable phonographs at your Bulova dealer today! Transistor radios as low as $24.95. Stereo sets as low as $79.95.

For the most advanced radio engineering and styling, see your Bulova dealer today!

1962 in Cinema and Film

From its peak in the mid-1940s, cinema attendance faced a steady decline as TV sets took pride of place in our living rooms. Cinemas struggled to stay profitable and by 1962 many were forced to close. The motion picture industry needed creative ways to win back audiences.

The new big screen formats of Cinerama, Cinemascope, and Visavision, ideal for sweeping historical epics, helped lure viewers back to the big screen. With the high costs of Hollywood productions and A-list talent, studios regularly took to filming abroad to reduce expenses. European and British cities were favored locations.

The musical comedy-drama *Gypsy* cast Hollywood A-lister Natalie Wood in the lead role. Although her voice had been dubbed in her previous musical *West Side Story* (1961), Wood sang all her own songs for *Gypsy*. The film was based on the memoirs of real-life burlesque performer Gypsy Rose Lee, with Lyrics by Stephen Sondheim.

Marlon Brando made cinema history by becoming the first actor to earn over $1 million for a single film, when he was cast in the lead role for the 1962 film remake of *Mutiny on the Bounty*.

1962 film debuts

Sally Field	Moon Pilot
Sydney Pollack	War Hunt
Bernardo Bertolucci	The Grim Reaper
Robert Duvall	To Kill a Mockingbird
Jackie Chan	Big and Little Wong Tin

* From en.wikipedia.org/wiki/1962_in_film.

Top Grossing Films of the Year

1	The Longest Day	20th Century Fox	$17,600,000
2	Lawrence of Arabia	Columbia Pictures	$16,700,000
3	The Music Man	Warner Bros.	$8,100,000
4	That Touch of Mink	Universal Pictures	$7,942,000
5	Mutiny on the Bounty	Metro-Goldwyn-Mayer	$7,410,000
6	To Kill a Mockingbird	Universal Pictures	$7,112,000
7	Hatari!	Paramount Pictures	$7,000,000
8	Gypsy	Warner Bros.	$6,000,000
9	Bon Voyage!	Walt Disney/Buena Vista	$5,000,000
=	The Interns	Columbia Pictures	$5,000,000
10	In Search of the Castaways	Walt Disney/Buena Vista	$4,900,000

* From en.wikipedia.org/wiki/1962_in_film by box office gross in the USA.

Based on Harper Lee's 1960 Pulitzer Prize-winning novel, the film *To Kill a Mocking Bird* was a critical success, winning 3 three Academy Awards and earning more than six times its budget at the box office. It has since been selected for preservation by the Library of Congress National Film Registry.

Hollywood favorites Cary Grant and Doris Day starred in the highly successful comedy-romance film *That Touch of Mink*. At 39 years old, Day was often referred to as "the professional virgin", always saving herself for the Mr. Right.

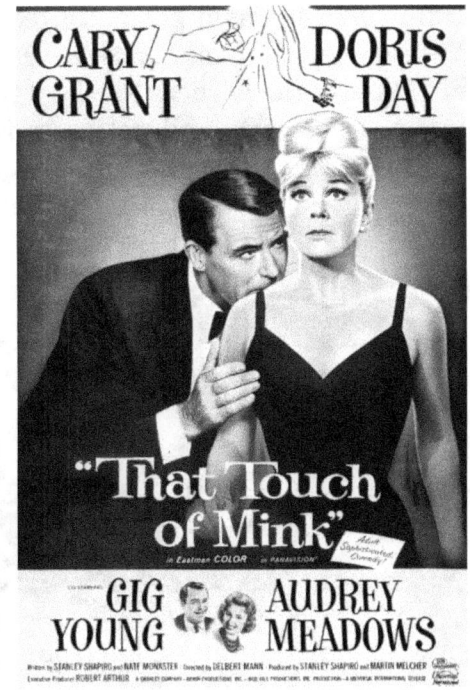

A Decade of Cinema Epics

The 1960s saw cinema studios take big risks with extravagant and spectacular epic films. Exotic locations, expensive sets, multiple A-list actors and casts of thousands ensured big box office ticket sales.

Peter O'Toole as Colonel T.E. Lawrence, in the historical epic *Lawrence of Arabia*, 1962.

The British epic *Lawrence of Arabia* is widely considered to be one of the greatest movies every made. With Peter O'Toole in the lead role, the cast included Omar Sharif, Anthony Quinn, and Alec Guinness. The film would win 7 of 10 nominations at the Academy Awards, and 4 of 5 nominations at the British Academy Film Awards.

Director Sir David Lean selected Super Panavision 70mm, to ensure the sweeping panoramas were shot in the largest frame possible. Although he wished to shoot entirely in the deserts of Jordan, increasing costs and delays caused by the difficult location forced filming to relocate to Spain.

In Jordan, the thousands of soldier extras were actual soldiers lent by King Hussein, while real Bedouin tribesmen were used in the desert scenes. Additionally, 450 horses and 150 camels were required for the *Charge on Aquaba* scene.

O'Toole with Omar Sharif as Sherif Ali ibn el Kharish.

At 3 hours 42 minutes long, not a single line is spoken by a woman.

The big budget, big box office war epic *The Longest Day* may have been the highest grossing film of 1962, however, unlike 2nd placed *Lawrence of Arabia*, it has failed to endure in our hearts and memories. The movie boasted 42 big name stars, including John Wayne, Henry Fonda, Robert Wagner, Sean Connery and Richard Burton.

The 3-hour-long film focused on the 1944 D-Day landings in Normandy. Multiple story lines provided each actor with very limited screen time, giving the film the aura of a fictionalized documentary.

Marlon Brando turned down the lead role in *Lawrence of Arabia*, selecting instead to play mutineer 1st Lt. Fletcher Christian in *Mutiny on the Bounty*. An untold number of difficulties plagued the film, including the lack of a finished script, and time and cost overruns. But the biggest obstacle was Brando himself, who refused to cooperate and behaved like a petulant child.

Trevor Howard as Captain Bligh (L) with Brando (R).

The movie fell far short of the $30 million needed to recoup its budget. The critics panned the film, in particular Brando's lackluster performance, destroying his star status. His acting career would stagnate until revived by *The Godfather* in 1972.

Advertisement

Here's a new cigarette...longer than King-size...and there's an honest-to-goodness smoker's reason behind its creation. York travels the smoke farther...farther...farther...to improve smoking taste. Yes, York uses its Imperial length instead of a filter to make rich tobaccos taste mild and smooth. A superbly luxurious blend of tobaccos for rich flavor. Imperial length for mild, smooth taste.

Never a flavor so rich...never a taste so smooth... **YORK**

Influential Cult Classics in Film

Dr. No, the first film in the *James Bond* series, was released in the UK on 5th Oct (United Artists, 1962). Based on the Ian Fleming novel of the same name, the low budget film launched to a mixed reception. It went on to become a cult classic, launching a steady stream of Bond films which are still being made today.

Sean Connery starred as 007, a role he would reprise for six further Bond films.

Stanly Kubrick's *Lolita* (MGM. 1962), based on Vladimir Nabokov's controversial novel of the same name, faced a barrage of censorship requirements from the Motion Picture Production Code. The psychological comedy-drama was given an X rating, despite Kubrick's toning down of the erotic relationship between the teenage Lolita and Humbert, her middle-aged stepfather.

The psychological political thriller *The Manchurian Candidate* (United Artists, 1962) was released during the Cuban Missile Crisis, while Cold War fears were at their highest. Starring Frank Sinatra, Laurence Harvey and Janet Leigh, the plot follows Chinese and Soviet agents planning to assassinate a US Presidential Nominee.

The film has since been preserved in the US National Film Registry by the Library of Congress. It was one of the first western movies to use martial arts in a fight scene.

Marilyn Monroe Life and Death   4th August 1962

Above: Publicity photo, 1953.
Below: On the set *of Something's Got to Give* (20th Century Fox, 1962).

From 1952-1962, Marilyn Monroe became one of Hollywood's most bankable stars. Her sex-bomb status is unrivaled to this day, and she remains an enduring icon of popular culture. Monroe's death on 4th Aug 1962, from an overdose of barbiturates, was ruled as probable suicide. However, countless conspiracy theories circulate proposing otherwise. Her naked body was found in her bedroom by her housekeeper and her psychiatrist. She was 36 years old.

Monroe had been suffering from substance abuse and mental problems for many years. She survived on a daily cocktail of alcohol, amphetamines, and barbiturates, which interfered with her ability to remember lines. As she struggled with low self-esteem, anxiety and chronic insomnia, she was often late to work and difficult to work with, if she turned up at all. Stints in hospital for heath care, depression or detox also upset filming schedules.

In early 1962, Monroe began filming *Something's Got to Give* for 20th Century Fox. She immediately took 6 weeks off due to illness, then traveled to New York to sing *Happy Birthday* to President Kennedy. On her return, Fox fired her, suing her for breach of contract. Although co-star Dean Martin insisted that she be reinstated, she would die before filming recommenced.

During her career, Monroe appeared in 29 films, including *The Seven Year Itch* (1955), *Gentlemen Prefer Blondes* (1953), *Bus Stop* (1956), and *The Misfits* (1961). She had married and divorced three times, without having any children.

The Pop Art of Andy Warhol

Since 1962, the humble soup can has become synonymous with the artist Andy Warhol.

Warhol first painted a series of 32 Campbell's soup cans (in 32 different flavors) for a one man show opening 9th July 1962 in LA, California. This low-key exhibition marked the West Coast debut of Pop Art.

A part of Warhol's Campbell soup can series. Now on display at the Museum of Modern Art, NY.

Below: Visitors to the Tate, London, view the Marilyn diptych, painted in 1962.
Bottom: Triple Elvis, 1962. Now on display at the San Francisco Museum of Modern Art.

Furious at the debasement of high art to the level of a supermarket shelf, critics were dubious of the art's value. Irving Blum, who curated the Warhol exhibition, purchased the entire set for $1,000.

The show closed one day before the death of Marilyn Monroe, inspiring Warhol to paint his Marilyn diptych, a 50-image contrast between Monroe's public persona and troubled private life.

Warhol's fame became attached to the celebrities whom he often painted. He also assembled an impressive collection of personal photographs of the New York socialite set he was known to party with.

Warhol preferred the silk screen technique for his art, also favored by Roy Lichtenstein, James Rosenquist and other Pop artists of the time.

Advertisement

This 10-speaker stereo can send...

high-fidelity music through your household wiring to...

any other room where you plug in this receiver speaker.

This 10-speaker stereo can send... high-fidelity music through your household wiring to... any other room where you plug in this receiver speaker.

General Electric calls this new idea a Home Music Distribution System. It works like this:

The console has a tiny FM transmitter, which broadcasts through regular household wiring. The portable 8" speaker is a receiver with its own loudness and tone controls.

Simply plug the portable unit into any standard 110-volt outlet. You'll enjoy radio or phonograph music from the console in any room you choose.

This innovation is on the Sutton, above, as well as the Barrington and Custom Decorator series.

The Sutton, by the way, is a superb instrument in itself. It combines ten speakers with a full 100 watts of music power amplification. An FM/AM/FM-Stereo tuner is standard. It comes in your choice of four authentic furniture styles—each in the appropriate genuine hardwood veneer.

The Sutton—<u>and</u> the ingenious Home Music Distribution System—are from a selection of fine console and portable stereos. <u>Hear</u> them at your General Electric dealer's.

Advertisement

Webcor Music Man stereo tape recorder

Play music... record music... learn music with this exciting new stereo tape recorder! The Music Man is an easy to operate self-contained stereo instrument–with two wide-range micro phones, two high fidelity speakers, and powerful dual-channel amplifier. Plays 2- or 4-track, in choice of three speeds, stereo or monaural. New music/language learning feature, Synchro-Track, enables you to add your own voice or instrument to previously recorded sound. Slide-Synchronizer jack even lets you record your own slide-show narration, complete with sound effects!

Webcor Music Man stereo phonograph

Play music... enjoy music–the way it was meant to be heard! This spunky, spanking new Music Man phonograph is styled for sound from inside out! Powerful dual-channel amplifier plays through three wide-range speakers, one in each of the detachable wings, and one in the center. Automatic 4-speed record changer plays all records–stereo and monaural–and even intermixes 7" and 12" LP's! Handsome, rugged carrying case in your choice of colors.

Who Were The Rat Pack?

They were known as The Rat Pack—a group of entertainer friends, who sang together, acted together, played hard and drank harder together. They had links to politicians, mafia, and Hollywood elite. In the early '60s, their favorite hangout was The Sands Hotel in Las Vegas, and between them, they transformed this dusty, desert town into the glamorous gambling and entertainment capitol of the world.

At its core, the Pack comprised: Frank Sinatra, Dean Martin, Sammy Davis Jnr, Peter Lawford and Joey Bishop. Their shows were broadcast on live TV, enticing other celebrities to perform in Las Vegas, turning it into a tourist destination town.

The Rat Pack were the kings of cool. They had swag, talent, energy, money and power. To see the Rat Pack at the Sands, a show with dinner and two drinks, cost a cool $5.95 per person.

At their peak, The Rat Pack made 5 films together including *Ocean's 11* (Warner Bros. 1960), *Sergeants Three* (United Artists, 1962), and *Four for Texas* (Warner Bros. 1963).

Below Left: Martin, Judy Garland & Sinatra.
Below Right: Sinatra, the leader of The Pack, recorded 14 albums during the years 1961 to 1963.

Musical Memories

American style rock 'n' roll had ruled the 1950s and early '60s, with movies, television, fashion, youth culture and attitudes worldwide influenced by this American export. By 1962, British home-grown rock artists were developing their own unique interpretation of the rock genre. And within a short few years, their international success—known as the British Invasion—would make The Rolling Stones, The Beatles, Cliff Richard, The Kinks, The Who, The Yardbirds, and others, household names.

24th Jan— The Beatles signed Brian Epstein as their manager. On 6th June 1962, the band played their first session at EMI's Abbey Road Studios in London, releasing their first single *Love Me Do/P.S. I Love You*, four months later in October.

29th May— Judy Garland's live recorded album *Judy at Carnegie Hall* won Album of the Year at the 4th Annual Grammy Awards. The two-disc album had spent 13 weeks at number one on the Billboard Charts.

12th Jul— The Rolling Stones played their first gig at London's Marquee Jazz Club. The six-month-old five-piece band merged blues and rock 'n' roll rhythms while developing their own grittier and edgier sounds. Only Mick Jagger and Keith Richards remain from the original line-up.

1962 Billboard Top 30 Songs

	Artist	Song Title
1	Acker Bilk	Stranger on the Shore
2	Ray Charles	I Can't Stop Loving You
3	Dee Dee Sharp	Mashed Potato Time
4	Bobby Vinton	Roses Are Red (My Love)
5	David Rose	The Stripper
6	Shelley Fabares	Johnny Angel
7	Little Eva	The Loco-Motion
8	The Sensations	Let Me In
9	Chubby Checker	The Twist
10	The Shirelles	Soldier Boy

Ray Charles, 1968.

Little Eva, 1962.

Shelley Fabares.

Chubby Checker, 1964.

	Artist	Song Title
11	Bruce Channel	Hey! Baby
12	Dion	The Wanderer
13	Gene Chandler	Duke of Earl
14	Freddy Cannon	Palisades Park
15	Neil Sedaka	Breaking Up Is Hard to Do
16	Claude King	Wolverton Mountain
17	Chubby Checker & Dee Dee Sharp	Slow Twistin'
18	Johnny Tillotson	It Keeps Right On a-Hurtin'
19	Mary Wells	The One Who Really Loves You
20	Elvis Presley	Good Luck Charm

Neil Sedaka, 1965.

The Shirelles, 1962.

	Artist	Song Title
21	Kenny Ball	Midnight in Moscow
22	Tommy Roe	Sheila
23	Sam Cooke	Twistin' the Night Away
24	The Orlons	The Wah-Watusi
25	Joey Dee and the Starliters	Peppermint Twist
26	Brenda Lee	Break It to Me Gently
27	The Marvelettes	Playboy
28	Nat King Cole	Ramblin' Rose
29	Brian Hyland	Sealed with a Kiss
30	Jay and the Americans	She Cried

* From the *Billboard* top 30 singles of 1962.

Dresses from the *National Bellas Hess* Home Shopping Catalog, Spring-Summer 1962.

Fashion Trends of the 1960s

The 1960s was a decade of fashion extremes driven by a vibrant and vocal youth, shifting social movements, rebelliousness and rejection of traditions. It was an exciting decade for fashion, with new trends that caught on and shifted quickly.

In the early '60s, fashion was content to continue the conservative classic style of the previous decade. The elegant sheath dress and tailored skirt-suits were still favored for day wear. And no lady would dare to venture out without her full ensemble of matching accessories. Gloves, hat, scarf, jewelry and stiletto or kitten-heel shoes were mandatory for any outing.

Christian Dior's voluptuous "New Look", favored throughout the 1950s, was still popular for cocktails or dinners. Less formal than the stiffer '50s styles, dresses retained their hour-glass shape but were now made with softer patterned fabrics. Skirts stayed long, full and very lady-like.

Television, cinema and magazine coverage kept us abreast of the latest in haute couture and street style, inspiring us with our favorite fashion icons.

Jacqueline Kennedy may have been the US first lady for only three years, but as first lady of fashion, her iconic status has endured till this day.

Jacqueline Kennedy, wearing her signature pearl necklace.

Always impeccably groomed, with perfectly applied make-up and coiffured hair, here are a few of her iconic looks:

- Tailored skirt-suit with three-quarter-sleeve box jacket and pill box hat in matching fabric.
- Sheath dress, low-heeled pump shoes and three-quarter gloves.
- A-line dress, long or short, with long gloves for evening.

After more than a decade of adherence to Dior's New Look, the first rumblings of change were being felt from Europe. The fashion houses of Italy were enticing us with bold new shapes and modern textiles.

Laminated silk shirt with elastic jersey pants by Emilio Schuberth. Layered form dress by Cesare Guidi.

Advertisement

Now Schick has invented the world's fastest home hairdryer!
(so relax and enjoy it)

Hair wet, or just set? Get into something comfortable—the new Schick Petite Salon Home Hairdryer. The heat is smooth and even—never a "hot spot." The bouffant hood fits over your largest rollers. It's the fastest—and quietest—of all home hairdryers! Cuts drying time to next-to-nothing! Travels light, too. For speed, comfort and ease, there's nothing like the new Schick Petite Salon..... so relax—and enjoy it!

SCHICK — the mark of quality

NEW SCHICK *Petite Salon* HAIRDRYER

Now Schick has invented the world's fastest home hairdryer!
(so relax and enjoy it)

Hair wet, or just set? Get into something comfortable–the new Schick Petite Salon Home Hairdryer. The heat is smooth and even–never a "hot spot." The bouffant hood fits over your largest rollers. It's the fastest–and quietest–of all home hairdryers! Cuts drying time to next-to-nothing! Travels light, too. For speed, comfort and ease, there's nothing like the new Schick Petite Salon..... so relax–and enjoy it!

Advertisement

I dreamed I stole the show in my Maidenform bra

Chansonette... best-loved Maidenform bra... now in care-free Dacron. Famous, fabulous combination of circular and spoke-stitched cups for superb fit, luscious curves. White, iced champagne, black. A, B, C cups. 2.50. D cup, 3.50.

The decade of the 1960s would belong to the British youth centered around London, who would soon capture the world's attention with their free spirits, energy, music, and style. The "British Invasion" exploded onto the world in the early '60s, introducing us to the "Mods", and later to the "Swinging Sixties". These movements defined the era and changed the world of fashion forever.

The Mods were clean-cut college boys who favored slim-fitting suits or short jackets over turtle-neck or buttoned up polo shirts. Pants were pipe-legged with no cuffs, worn over pointed polished shoes or ankle boots. Mods were obsessed with Italian fashion, French haircuts, and alternative music.

For the girls, London designer Mary Quant created fashion for the young and free-spirited woman. Quant invented the mini skirt, worn with bold colored or patterned tights. Her boutique featured simple short dresses in bold or floral patterns.

By the mid-'60s, Quant championed hot pants for women. Her experimental use of new materials was revolutionary. She created synthetic dresses, patent plastic boots, shiny PVC raincoats and bold colorful jewelry, handbags and accessories.

By the mid-'60s the world would be captivated by the unstoppable energy of London's Swinging Sixties. The term captured the modern fun-loving hedonism of swinging London. It was the era of the British supermodel–tall, skinny, leggy young ladies, with enormous eyes and descriptive names. Jean Shrimpton, Twiggy, and Penelope Tree were in-demand icons world-wide. The British supermodels broke with the aristocratic look of earlier-generation models, redefining beauty standards for a younger, more care-free generation.

Penelope Tree for *Vogue,* October 1967.

Twiggy for *Italian Vogue*, July 1967.

Twiggy various photo shoots.

Jean Shrimpton for *Australian Women's Weekly*, August 1965.

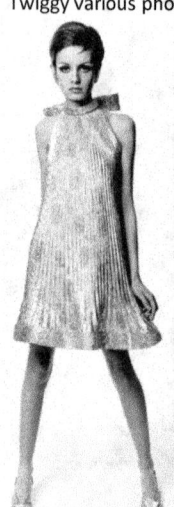

As the fashion and attitudes of swinging London spread to America and other parts of the world, the sub-culture became commercialized on a mass scale and began to loose its vitality. The Swinging Sixties morphed into the psychedelic rock and early hippie movements.

Led by musicians such as The Beatles, The Beach Boys, Pink Floyd and The Who, and fuelled by the widespread use of marijuana and LSD, psychedelic fashion became an expression of the hallucinogenic experience with bright colors, swirling patterns and kaleidoscopic floral designs.

From The Beatles *Magical Mystery Tour,* 1967.

The psychedelic rock movement petered out by the end of the 1960s, but the hippie generation was only just beginning. Hippies would drive fashion forward, well into the next decade.

Advertisement

Avon For Men   She enjoys choosing it...he enjoys using it!

Avon presents a man's world of good grooming in handsome new red and white packaging. Great news is Avon's refreshing After Shave—After Shower Spray with the crisp, spicy scent men like. And Avon brings a wide selection of shaving creams—lather, brushless, aerosol—after shave lotions, hair care and deodorant products to make a man feel perfectly groomed all day.

Avon calling...a visit with your gracious, thoughtful Avon Representative who brings to your home good grooming products for the man in your life, and cosmetics for the whole family.

I leave it to the girls... And rent my car from Hertz

Let the girls go to town in the family car–it's so easy to rent *your* car from Hertz. Next time you need a car for business or pleasure, just call your local Hertz office to reserve a new Chevrolet (or Pontiac, Buick, Oldsmobile, Cadillac or other fine car) for an hour, day, weekend or week. The low Hertz rate includes everything– insurance, gas and oil (even if you buy it on the road)!

Let Hertz put you in the driver's seat!

Katherine Johnson NASA's Computer

John H. Glenn Jr. may have been the first American to orbit the earth when he circled three times in February 1962, but exactly how did he get there?

In the early '60s, NASA still relied on human brainpower to perform complex mathematical calculations. These mathematicians were known as "computers". Katherine Johnson joined NASA in 1953, working for the West Area team—an African American women's team known as "Colored Computers".

At that time, engineering was "men's work", while computing was "women's work". Within 5 years, Johnson broke down barriers, when she was moved to the Spacecraft Controls Branch—a team of all-white, male engineers.

Johnson was responsible for calculating the launch window, trajectory, and navigation charts for Alan Shepard's 1961 suborbital flight. But the task for which she is best remembered, was for providing the calculations needed on Glenn's 1962 orbital flight from take off to touch down. Reluctant to trust the data from NASA's new IBM computer, Glenn asked for Johnson, saying, "If she says they're good, then I'm ready to go."

Johnson's role in NASA, and that of the Colored Computers of the '50s and '60s, remained largely unknown. In 2016, 20th Century Fox's critically acclaimed film *Hidden Figures* brought their story to the world. Johnson worked at NASA for 33 years. In 2015 she was awarded the *Presidential Medal of Freedom* by President Barack Obama. Two NASA facilities have since been named in her honor.

Science and Medicine

26th Apr– Ranger IV became the first American spacecraft to reach another celestial body when it crash-landed on the moon. No data was transmitted back to Earth due to failure of the on-board computers.

14th Jun– Ten European countries signed an agreement to form the *European Space Research Organisation,* (now the *European Space Agency),* with the goal of conducting joint scientific research in space. The Agency now has 17 countries as member states.

10th Jul– AT&T launched into orbit the world's first commercial communications satellite. The next day, Telstar 1 beamed a live television broadcast from the US to the UK. Within two weeks, full-length TV programs were being broadcast.

14th Dec– US spacecraft Mariner 2 flew past Venus, becoming the first probe to successfully transmit data from another planet.

22nd Nov– UK surgeon John Charnley performed the world's first successful total hip replacement operation in Wrightington Hospital, UK.

1962– Albert Sabin's Oral Polio Vaccine was licensed for public use and given to millions of children.

Advertisement

"Why we chose the NCR 390 Computer." –The Detroit Teachers Credit Union.

"Nearly one year was spent in studying systems before the decision was made to use the NCR 390 Computer. As the world's largest teachers credit union, we were excited by the big computers, but we realized that they were priced too high to give us an economical operation on our particular needs.

"The first requirement for our need, as it is for any financial institution, is that transactions be recorded accurately. The program of using the NCR Class 41 Window Receipting Machines coupled with a punched paper tape recorder proved most practical.

"The second requirement was to have a system that was economical. Studying the work performance of the 390 system showed that this achievement could be an early expectation. Even with a by-weekly peak load of many times the average daily transactions, all ledgers are now updated quickly and accurately. And, we save over 2,500 overtime hours computing and posting annual dividends.

"In summary, the ability of the 390 to post ledger records that can be read by people as well as the computer itself, has enabled us to retain our traditionally valuable history records. And it is interesting to note that our own people were able to program the computer after a relatively brief training period."

Fred Dean, Assistant Treasurer.

Also in Sports

24th Jan– Jackie Robinson became the first African American elected to the *Baseball Hall of Fame*. He was celebrated for bringing an end to racial segregation in Major League Baseball when he was signed with the Brooklyn Dodgers in 1947.

17th June– Brazil defended their FIFA World Cup title, winning the final against Czechoslovakia in Santiago, Chile. 56 teams entered the competition, remembered as the most violent tournament in football history. Scuffles between players broke out during several matches, including the infamous "Battle of Santiago" match between Chile and Italy, during which police were called to intervene on the field four times.

15th Jul– Defending champion Jacques Anquetil of France won the 49th Tour de France. He would become the first cyclist to win five tours (1957, 1961-'64). His 1962 speed record stood until 1981.

17th Jun– Jack Nicklaus won his first major title at the US Open in Oakmont Country Club in Pennsylvania. During his long career he would become one of golf's greatest, winning 117 professional tournaments including 18 majors.

22nd Nov– The 1962 British Empire and Commonwealth Games began in Perth, Australia, with 863 athletes from 35 nations competing. Australia took home the most medals, with England placing second, and New Zealand placing third.

1962– Rod Laver of Australia won the Grand Slam (four major titles), winning a further 18 titles for a season total of 22. He would go on to become one of tennis' greatest players, ranking #1 for seven straight years from 1964 to 1970.

Other News from 1962

14th Jun– "The Boston Strangler" sexually assaulted and killed his first victim. His killing-by-strangulation spree continued for 18 months. Albert DeSalvo, arrested on a separate rape charge, confessed to all 13 murders.

4th Feb– For the first time in 400 years, Mercury, Venus, Mars, Saturn, Jupiter, the sun and the moon all aligned (within 16 degrees).

21st Feb– Margot Fonteyn and Rudolf Nureyev first danced together, in a Royal Ballet performance of *Giselle*. Their partnership is still considered one of the greatest in ballet history.

21st Apr– The Century 21 Exposition (Seattle World's Fair) opened in Seattle, Washington. 10 million people attended the 6-month fair, revitalizing Seattle's economy and resulting in many notable buildings. The theme of *Space, Science, and the Future* foretold an optimistic future with technology at its core.

1st Jun– German-Austrian SS officer Adolf Eichmann was executed by hanging in Israel. The Holocaust leader, responsible for the "Final Solution to the Jewish Question" had been found guilty of war crimes.

1st Mar– The first Kmart department store opened in Garden City, Michigan.

2nd Jul– The first Wal-Mart, known as Wal-Mart Discount City, opened in Rogers, Arkansas.

Hostages welcomed home by the President and First Lady Kennedy.

24th Dec– 1,113 hostages, captured in Cuba during the 1961 Bay of Pigs invasion, were exchanged for $53 million in food and medicine.

5th Jun– The Spider-Man superhero, created by Stan Lee and Steve Ditko, made its debut for Marvel in the comic book *Amazing Fantasy* issue #15.

1962– Algeria, Burundi, Jamaica, Western Samoa, Uganda, and Trinidad and Tobago gained independence.

3rd Dec– Edith S. Sampson was appointed to the Municipal Court of Chicago, becoming the first African American female judge. She had also been the first African American to represent the US at the United Nations when she was appointed to the General Assembly in 1950.

1st Mar– A Boeing 707 American Airlines plane crashed on takeoff at New York International Airport. Its rudder separated from its tail. All passengers and crew on board died.

22nd May– A Continental Airlines domestic flight exploded and crashed in a Missouri field, killing all on board. The cause was deemed a suicide bombing committed as insurance fraud.

3rd Jun– A Boeing 707 Air France chartered plane carrying cultural and civic leaders of Atlanta, Georgia, overran the runway at Orly Airport, Paris. 130 of 132 passengers were killed.

22nd Jun– A Boeing 707 Air France plane crashed into a mountain and exploded on descent into Guadeloupe. All 113 on board were killed.

Sociable? Very. New! 6 party shapes in one package!
New Sociables shape up in 6 ways to every snack that ever made a party. With dips, spreads, plain cheese or fancy caviar... they're the tastiest! Sociables Crackers are so snappy, so nutlike-savory you'll love them by the handful, too. So serve 'em up soon... at special or simple doings. They'll do you a big party favor!

Advertisement

Clever on Sunday

Tupperware makes it possible: You can set out a fine Sunday lunch and have time to enjoy the papers, too. Here's how. Cook earlier in the week, store in Tupperware, serve on Sunday. Tupperware's patented airtight seal will keep your food delectably fresh. And these unique plastic containers are so colorful, you'll bring them right to the table for serving. All very relaxed. You can relax when you *buy* Tupperware, too. Come to a Tupperware Home Party or have one of your own. Phone the local Tupperware distributor for the name of your nearest dealer, or write Department L1, Tupperware Home Parties Inc., Orlando, Fla.

Clever on Sunday

Tupperware makes it possible: You can set out a fine Sunday lunch and have time to enjoy the papers, too. Here's how. Cook earlier in the week, store in Tupperware, serve on Sunday. Tupperware's patented airtight seal will keep your food delectably fresh. And those unique plastic containers are so colorful, you'll bring them right to the table for serving. All very relaxed. You can relax when you buy Tupperware, too. Come to a Tupperware Home Party or have one of your own. Phone the local Tupperware distributor for the name of your nearest dealer, or write Department L1, Tupperware Home Parties Inc. Orlando, Fla.

Famous People Born in 1962

17th Jan– Jim Carrey, Canadian-American actor.

6th Feb– Axl Rose [William Bailey], American singer-songwriter (Guns & Roses).

7th Feb– Garth Brooks, American country singer.

11th Feb– Sheryl Crow, American singer-songwriter.

22nd Feb– Steve Irwin, Australian naturalist & TV personality (The Crocodile Hunter, d. 2006).

1st Mar– Russell Coutts, New Zealand yachtsman (America's Cup 5x winner).

2nd Mar– Jon Bon Jovi [John Bongiovi], American singer-songwriter.

12th Mar– Darryl Strawberry, American MLB right fielder (8x All Star).

18th Mar– Mike Rowe, American TV personality (Dirty Jobs).

21st Mar– Matthew Broderick, American actor.

21st Mar– Rosie O'Donnell, American comedienne & actress.

1st Apr– Phillip Schofield, British TV personality.

12th May– Emilio Estevez, American actor.

17th May– Craig Ferguson, Scottish actor, writer, TV personality & comedian.

19th Jun– Paula Abdul, American singer-songwriter, choreographer & TV personality.

27th Jun– Michael Ball, British singer & actor.

3rd Jul– Tom Cruise, American actor.

31st Jul– Wesley Snipes, American actor.

6th Aug– Michelle Yeoh, Malaysian actress.

10th Aug– Suzanne Collins, American author (The Hunger Games Trilogy).

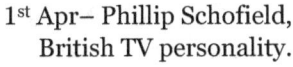

16th Aug– Steve Carell, American actor & comedian.

28th Aug– David Fincher, American film & TV director and producer.

17th Sep– Baz Luhrmann, Australian film director.

3rd Oct– Tommy Lee [Bass], American drummer (Mötley Crüe).

13th Oct– Kelly Preston, American actress, (d.2020).

11th Nov– Demi Moore [Guynes], American actress.

12th Nov– Naomi Wolf, American author & feminist.

19th Nov– Jodie Foster, American actress.

28th Nov– Jon Stewart [Jonathan Stuart Leibowitz], American Comedian (The Daily Show).

8th Dec– Steve Elkington, Australian golfer (10x PGA titles).

9th Dec– Felicity Huffman, American actress.

22nd Dec– Ralph Fiennes, English actor.

24th Dec– Kate Spade, American fashion designer, (d.2018).

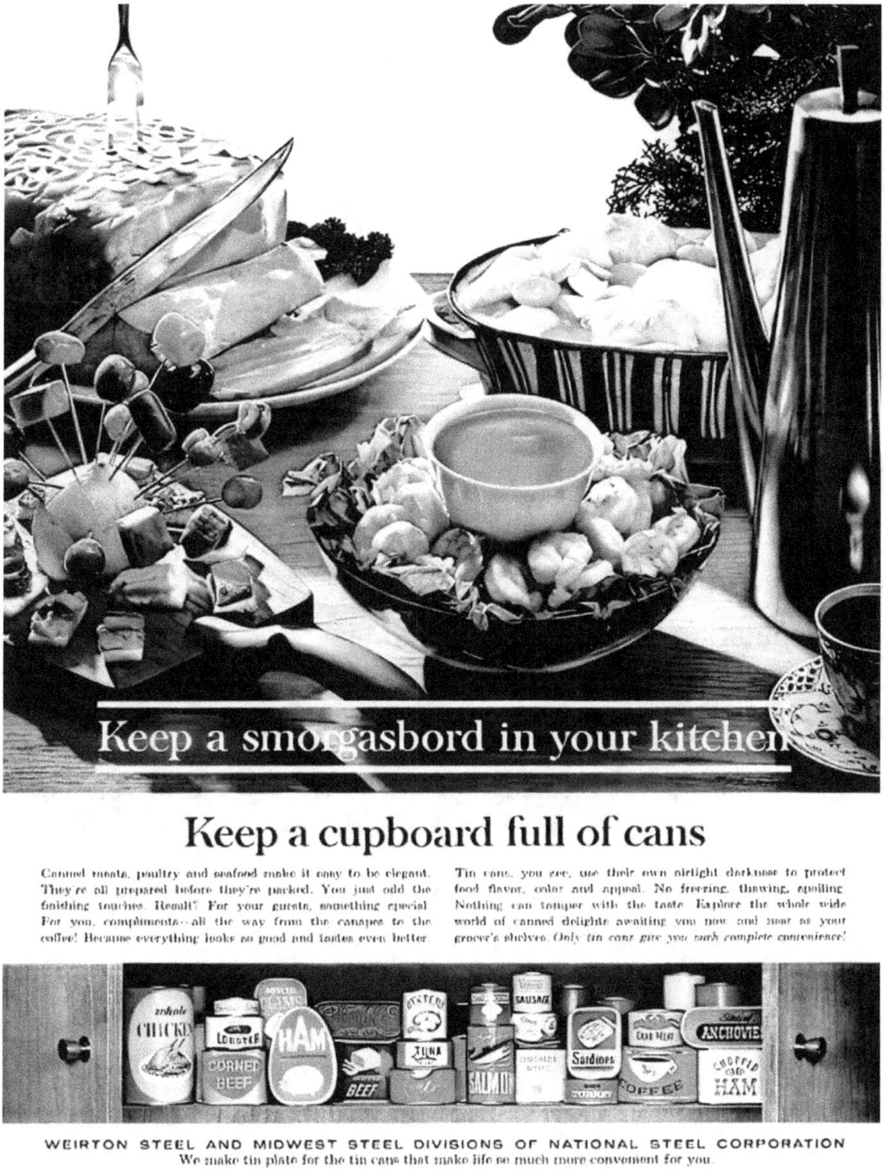

Advertisement

Keep a cupboard full of cans

WEIRTON STEEL AND MIDWEST STEEL DIVISIONS OF NATIONAL STEEL CORPORATION
We make tin plate for the tin cans that make life so much more convenient for you.

Keep a smorgasbord in your kitchen
Keep a cupboard full of cans

Canned meats, poultry and seafood make it easy to be elegant. They're all prepared before they're packed. You just add the finishing touches. Result? For your guests, something special. For you, compliments—all the way from the canapes to the coffee! Because everything looks so good and tastes even better.

Tin cans, you see, use their own airtight darkness to protect food flavor, color and appeal. No freezing, thawing, spoiling. Nothing can tamper with the taste. Explore the whole wide world of canned delights awaiting you now and near as your grocer's shelves. *Only tin cans give you such complete convenience!*

1962 in Numbers

Census Statistics [1]:

- Population of the world   3.15 billion
- Population in the United States   192.31 million
- Population in the United Kingdom   53.11 million
- Population in Canada   18.59 million
- Population in Australia   10.64 million
- Average age for marriage of women   20.3 years old
- Average age for marriage of men   22.7 years old
- Average family income USA $5,800 per year
- Unemployment rate USA   5.5 %

Costs of Goods [2]:

- Average home — $19.580
- Average new car — $3,125
- New Pontiac Grand Prix — $3,500
- A gallon of gasoline — $0.31
- Apples — $0.39 per 3 pounds
- Butter — $0.63 per pound
- Sugar — $0.49 per 5 pounds
- Beef, rib steaks — $0.79 per pound
- Bacon — $0.69 per pound
- Fish, cod fillet — $0.69 per pound
- Fresh Eggs — $0.32 per dozen
- Oranges, Valencia — $0.29 for 10
- Film developing, Kodacolor — $2.85 for 12 pictures
- Drive-in movie — $1.00 per car

---

1 Figures taken from worldometers.info/world-population, US National Center for Health Statistics, Divorce and Divorce Rates US (cdc.gov/nchs/data/series/sr_21/sr21_029.pdf) and United States Census Bureau, Historical Marital Status Tables (census.gov/data/tables/time-series/demo/families/marital.html).
2 Figures from thepeoplehistory.com, mclib.info/reference/local-history & dqydj.com/historical-home-prices/.

Advertisement

Advertisement

If you smoke for pleasure and not just from habit, smoke the cigarette that really satisfies.
21 Great Tobaccos make 20 Wonderful Smokes!!

Pleasure's True. Twenty-one great vintage tobaccos are grown mild, aged mild and blended mild—*not* filtered mild in every Chesterfield King.

Pleasure's Long. Nothing satisfies like the great taste of great tobaccos *blended* mild. And you get King-size flavor in the long, long length of the King.

Pleasure's Filter-Free. The goodness of 21 great tobaccos is not lost in a filter—*all* the flavor gets home to you. Enjoy the true satisfaction of this true cigarette.

The great tobaccos are in both Regular Chesterfield and Chesterfield King.

They Satisfy

These words first appeared in print in the year 1962.

TRENDY

Optical Fiber

Business Class

multiscreen

miniskirt

COMMAND MODULE

satellite dish

GIGAWATT

log on

OVAL OFFICE

decathlete

zip-code

can of worms

buckle up

GET-GO

MIXED-MEDIA

HEAT SHIELD

*From merriam-webster.com/time-traveler/1962.

A heartfelt plea from the author:

I sincerely hope you enjoyed reading this book and that it brought back many fond memories from the past.

Success as an author has become increasingly difficult with the proliferation of **AI generated** copycat books by unscrupulous sellers. They are clever enough to escape copyright action and use dark web tactics to secure paid-for **fake reviews**, something I would never do.

Hence I would like to ask you—I plead with you—the reader, to leave a star rating or review on Amazon. This helps make my book discoverable for new readers, and helps me to compete fairly against the devious copycats.

If this book was a gift to you, you can leave stars or a review on your own Amazon account, or you can ask the gift-giver or a family member to do this on your behalf.

I have enjoyed researching and writing this book for you and would greatly appreciate your feedback.

Best regards,
Bernard Bradforsand-Tyler.

Please leave a
book review/rating at:

https://bit.ly/1962-reviews

Or scan the QR code:

Flashback books make the perfect gift- see the full range at

https://bit.ly/FlashbackSeries

Image Attributions

Photographs and images used in this book are reproduced courtesy of the following:

Page 6 – From *Better Homes and Gardens* Magazine Oct 1962, (PD image).*
Page 8 – Detail of Formica advertisement, from *Better Homes and Gardens* Magazine, Oct 1962, (PD image).*
Page 9 – Detail of Edison Electric Institute ad, from *Readers Digest* Magazine, April 1964, (PD image).*
Page 10 – From *Life* Magazine 2nd Mar 1962.
Source: books.google.com/books?id=kE0EAAAAMBAJ&printsec (PD image).*
Page 11 – From *Life* Magazine 21st Dec 1962.
Source: books.google.com/books?id=m0oEAAAAMBAJ&printsec (PD image).*
Page 12 – Image cropped from Edison Electric Institute advertisement in *Life* Magazine, 7th Apr 1961. Source: books.google.com/ books?id=-FEEAAAAMBAJ&printsec. Pre-1978, no copyright mark (PD image).*
Page 13 – Civil rights marches, Washington DC. 28th Aug 1963, from US Library of Congress's Prints and Photographs div. Source: loc.gov/item/2003654395/ by Leffler, Warren K. and loc.gov/resource/ppmsca.37245/ by Trikosko, Marion S. (PD).
Page 14 – Still image from the video *Life In 60s* Britain by Chaz Mork. Source: youtube.com/watch?v=pH0kvxCfvG8. Videographer unknown. This is a low-resolution image for information only, reproduced under fair use terms. It is believed that this image will not devalue the ability of the copyright holder to profit from the original work.
Page 15 – Piccadilly Circus, circa 1963. Creator unknown. Pre-1978, no copyright mark (PD image).
Page 16 – From *Life* Magazine 3rd Aug 1962.
Source: books.google.com/books?id=JU4EAAAAMBAJ&printsec (PD image).*
Page 17 – Lady on a London Bus, 1960. Photographer unknown. Pre-1978, no copyright mark (PD image). – The Beatles on the Ed Sullivan Show, 9th Feb 1964, by CBS. Source: commons.wikimedia.org/wiki/File: Beatles_with_Ed_Sullivan. jpg. Pre-1978, no copyright mark (PD image).
Page 18 – From *Life* Magazine 12th Jan 1962.
Source: books.google.com/books?id=nU0EAAAAMBAJ&printsec (PD image).*
Page 19 – Pontiac from *Life* Magazine, 12th Jan 1962. Source: books.google.com/books?id=nU0EAAAAMBAJ& printsec. (PD image).* – Steaknshake, source: web.archive.org/web/20080801225201/http://www. steaknshake.com/history.asp. Pre-1978, no copyright mark (PD image).
Page 20 – 1962 Chevrolet print advertisement, source ebay.com (PD image).* – Buick Special advertisement, from *Life* Magazine, 12th Jan 1962. Source: books.google.com/books?id=nU0EAAAAMBAJ&printsec (PD image).* – Mercury Comet, from *Life* Magazine, 9th Feb 1962.
Source: books.google.com/books?id=gE0EAAAAMBAJ&printsec (PD image).*
Page 21 – 1962 Fiat 1100 Series Advertisement from *Time* Magazine 9th Feb 1962.
Source: flickr.com/photos/91591049@ N00/23449288900/ by SenseiAlan. Attribution 4.0 International (CC BY 4.0). – 1962 Renault R4, source: flickr.com/photos/ hugo90/2120835097/ by JOHN LLOYD. Attribution 4.0 International (CC BY 4.0). – Volkswagen (1961) from *Life* Mag 5th May.
Source: books.google.com/books?id=qE8EAAAAMBAJ&printsec (PD image).*
Page 22 – From *Newsweek*, 22nd Jan 1962.
Source: flickr.com/photos/91591049@N00/21002105894/. Attribution 4.0 International (CC BY 4.0).
Page 23 – '62 Corvair Monza print advertisement, source: eBay.com (PD image).*
Page 24 – From *Life* Magazine Motorola advert, 6th Oct 1961.
Source: books.google.com/books?id=01MEAAAAMBAJ&printsec (PD image).*
Page 25 – *The Lucy Show* screen still by Desilu / CBS, 6th Jan 1963.** Source: commons.wikimedia.org/wiki/ Category: The_Lucy_ Show. – Van Dyke and Moore 1961, publicity image by CBS, source: en.wikipedia.org/wiki/The_Dick_Van_ Dyke_Show. Pre-1978, no copyright mark (PD image).
Page 26 – From *Life* Magazine, 9th Feb 1962.
Source: books.google.com/books?id=gE0EAAAAMBAJ&printsec (PD image).*
Page 27 – *The Virginian* publicity photo by Revue Studio, 1962. Source: en.wikipedia.org/wiki/The_Virginian _(TV_series). – Williams hosting the Grammy Awards 1963. Source: commons.wikimedia.org/wiki/ Category:Andy_Williams. – Borngine in *McHale's Navy* 1962. Source: commons.wikimedia.org/wiki/ Category:McHale%27s_Navy. – *The Tonight Show* debut 31st Dec 1962 by NBC. Source: en.wikipedia.org/wiki/ The_Tonight_Show_Starring_Johnny_ Carson. All images this page Pre-1978, no copyright mark (PD image).
Page 28 – From *Life* Magazine 2nd Feb 1962.
Source: books.google.com/books?id=k00EAAAAMBAJ&printsec (PD image).*
Page 29 – Operation Dominic Swordfish, 11th May 1962, and Operation Storax Sedan, 5th July 1962. Both photos by the Federal government of the USA, from the National Nuclear Security Administration Nevada Site Office Photo Library (PD image).
Page 30 – Images source: commons.wikimedia.org/wiki/Category:Cuban_Missile_Crisis. These photos are the property of the US Government and are in the public domain.
Page 31 – Gagarin, source: tass.com/society/899827 by Valentin Cheredintsev. Pre-1978, no copyright mark (PD image).
Page 54 – National Bellas Hess Home Shopping Catalog, Spring-Summer 1962. (PD image).*
Page 55 –2-piece suit from the Wool Bureau advertisement, from Life Magazine, 8th Feb 1960. Source: books. google.com/books?id=-EoEAAAAMBAJ&printsec. (PD image).* – Tea dresses from La Pastorale catalogue, Summer 1962. Source: likesoldclothes.tumblr.com/search/1962/. Pre-1978, no copyright mark (PD image). – Glenn, Image Credit: NASA. Source: nasa.gov/content/astronaut-john-glenn-at-cape-Canaveral (PD image).

Page 32 – Green Beret in Vietnam, 1961, from Life Magazine. Source: sofrep.com/news/jfk-sends-400-green-beret-special-advisors-may-1961-begin-vietnam-involvement/. Pre-1978, no copyright mark (PD image).
– US choppers, 1962, from Life Magazine. Source: 1960sdaysofrage.wordpress.com/2017/10/24/operation-chopper/. Pre-1978, no copyright (PD image).
Page 33 – From *Newsweek* 14th May 1962.
Source: flickr.com/photos/91591049@N00/21921961428 /. Attribution 4.0 International (CC BY 4.0).
Page 34 – From *Life* Magazine 8th Jun 1962.
Source: books.google.com/books?id=BVIEAAAAMBAJ&printsec (PD image).*
Page 35 – Meredith escorted onto Ole Miss. Source: US Library of Congress Prints and Photographs Division, reproduction number: LC-DIG-ppmsca-04292. – US Army trucks, by Jerry Huff, United Press International. Source: US Library of Congress Prints and Photographs division under the digital ID cph.3c35522. These photos are the property of the US Government and are in the public domain.
Page 36 –Mandela, source: commons.wikimedia.org/wiki/Category:Nelson_Mandela. Attribution-ShareAlike (CC BY-SA 2.0).
Page 37 – Indo-Sino war photos from Oct-Nov 1962, creators unknown. Sources: indiatoday.in/education-today/gk-current-affairs/story/india-china-war-of-1962-839077-2016-11-21 and commons.wikimedia.org/wiki/Category:Sino-Indian_War. /. Pre-1978, no copyright mark (PD image).
Page 38 – From *Life* Magazine, 2nd Nov 1962.
Source: books.google.com/books?id=n0oEAAAAMBAJ&printsec (PD image).*
Page 39 – From *Life* Magazine, 11th May 1962.
Source: books.google.com/books?id=1k0EAAAAMBAJ&printsec (PD image).*
Page 40 – Screen stills from *Mutiny on the Bounty*, MGM 1962**, and *Gypsy*, Warner Bros. 1962.**
Page 41 – *To Kill a Mocking Bird* movie poster, by Universal Pictures 1962.**
Source: en.wikipedia.org/wiki/To_Kill_a_Mockingbird_ (film). – *Gypsy* movie poster, Warner Bros. 1962.**
Source: en.wikipedia.org/wiki/Gypsy_ (1962_film).
Page 42 & 43 – Screen stills from *Lawrence of Arabia*, Horizon Pictures and Columbia Pictures, 1962.** – Screen still poster from *The Longest Day*, Darryl F. Zanuck/ 20th Century Fox, 1962.** – Screen still from *Mutiny on the Bounty,* MGM, 1962.**
Page 44 – From *Life* Magazine, 4th May 1962.
Source: books.google.com/books?id=3U4EAAAAMBAJ&printsec (PD image).*
Page 45 – Screen stills from Dr. No, Eon-United Artists 1962**. – Promotional image for Lolita by MGM. 1962,** and The Manchurian Candidate by United Artists, 1962.**
Page 46 – Monroe studio publicity photo for the cover of Photoplay magazine, 1953. Source: commons. wikimedia.org/ wiki/Category:Marilyn_Monroe_in_1953. – Monroe on the set of Something's Got to Give in 1962 from Eureka Humboldt Standard, 7th Aug 1962. Source: commons.wikimedia.org/wiki/Category:Marilyn_ Monroe_in_1962. Both images pre-1978, no copyright mark (PD images).
Page 47 – Detail from Warhol's 32 Campbell's soup cans. Image is reproduced under terms of Fair Use, as it is significant to the article and is rendered in low resolution to avoid piracy. It is believed that this image will not in any way limit the ability of the copyright owners to sell their product. – Marilyn Diptych, 1962. Source: flickr.com/photos/perspective/ 47435926571/. Attribution-ShareAlike 4.0 International (CC BY-SA 4.0) – Triple Elvis, 1963. Source: flickr.com/photos/ nat507/27587725394/. Attribution (CC BY-SA 4.0).
Page 48 – From *Life* Magazine 5th Oct 1962.
Source: books.google.com/books?id=eVUEAAAAMBAJ&printsec (PD image).*
Page 49 – From *Life* Magazine 7th Sep 1962.
Source: books.google.com/books?id=-k0EAAAAMBAJ&printsec (PD image).*
Page 50 – Movie poster for Ocean's 11, by Warner Bros, 1960.** – Sinatra publicity photo by CBS. 1966, and Martin, Garland, Sinatra from *The Judy Garland Show* in 1962.**
Source: commons.wikimedia.org/wiki/Category:Frank_Sinatra.
Page 51 – The Beatles in Milan, 1965. Source: it.wikipedia.org/wiki/File:Beatles_duomo. Photographer unknown. Pre-1978, no copyright mark (PD image). – Judy Garland, by Lindeboom, Henk / Anefo for Nationaal Archief Noord-Holland. Access number 2.24.01.03. 8th Dec 1960. Source: nationaalarchief.nl/onderzoeken/fotocollectie/a9c22aac-d0b4-102d-bcf8-003048976d84. CC0 1.0 Universal PD image). – The Rolling Stones at Schiphol, Amsterdam, 8th Aug 1964 by Gelderen, Hugo van/Anefo. Source: commons.wikimedia.org/wiki/Category:The_Rolling_Stones_in_1964. Pre-1978. no mark (PD image).
Page 52 – Ray Charles by Koch, Eric / Anefo, 5th Oct 1968. Source: commons.wikimedia.org/wiki/ Category:Ray_Charles. – Little Eva, unknown author, circa 1962. – Shelley Fabares, unknown date and author. – Chubby Checker, unknown author, photo 1964. Source: commons.wikimedia.org/wiki/File:Chubby_ Checker_1964.jpg. All images this page are Pre-1978 no copyright mark (PD image).
Page 53 – Neil Sedaka publicity photo, 1965. Source: commons.wikimedia.org/wiki/Category:Neil_Sedaka. Pre-1978 no copyright mark (PD image). – The Shirelles, Billboard ad by *Scepter Records*, 24th Nov 1962.**
Source: commons.wikimedia.org/wiki/Category:The_Shirelles#/media/File:The_Shirelles_1962.jpg.
Page 56 – Jacqueline Kennedy in the Diplomatic Reception Room, 5th Dec 1961 White House. Source: commons.wikimedia.org/wiki/Category:Jacqueline_Kennedy_Onassis_in_1961. Property of the US Government in the public domain. – Kennedy at the Elysee Palace, France, 31st May 1961, from the JFK Library. Source: commons.wikimedia.org/wiki/File:President_De_Gaulle_stands_between_President_ Kennedy_and_Mrs._Kennedy_on_the_steps_of_the_Elysee_Palace.jpg (PD image). – Jaqueline Kennedy at the US Embassy, New Delhi, March 12-21, 1962. Source: flickr.com/photos/54323860@N06/6914524677. Attribution-NoDerivatives 4.0 International (CC BY-ND 4.0).

– Italian fashions from 1960, creator unknown. Source: moda.com/fashion-history/60s-italian-fashion-1.shtml, reproduced under terms of Fair Use. Images here are significant to the article and are rendered in low resolution to avoid piracy. It is believed that these images will not in any way limit the ability of the copyright owners to sell their product.

Page 57 – From *Life* Magazine 7th Dec 1962.
Source: books.google.com/books?id=oEoEAAAAMBAJ&printsec (PD image).*

Page 58 – From *Life* Magazine 5th Oct 1962.
Source: books.google.com/books?id=eVUEAAAAMBAJ&printsec (PD image).*

Page 59 – Photo Mods of the early 1960s. Source unknown. Pre-1978 (PD image). – Models in Mary Quant mini dresses, creator unknown. Source: thedabbler.co.uk/2012/10/granny-takes-a-trip-back-in-time/. Pre-1978 (PD image). – Mary Quant, 16 December 1966. Source: commons.wikimedia.org/wiki/File:Mary_Quant_in_a_minidress_(1966).jpg by Jac. de Nijs / Anefo. Image from the Nationaal Archief, the Dutch National Archives, licensed under the Creative Commons Attribution-Share Alike 3.0 Netherlands.

Page 60 – Penelope Tree, photographer Richard Avedon for Vogue Oct 1967. – Jean Shrimpton for Australian Vogue August 1965, Twiggy for Italian Vogue, July 1967, and various photo of Twiggy, dates, photographers, source unknown. Images reproduced this page under terms of Fair Use are used sparingly for information only, are significant to the article created and are rendered in low resolution to avoid piracy. It is believed that these images will not in any way limit the ability of the copyright owners to sell their product.

Page 61 – Models wear fashions from the late '60s. Creators unknown. Pre-1978, (PD images). – The Beatles. Source: commons.wikimedia.org/wiki/File:The_Beatles_magical_mystery_tour.jpg. Attrib 3.0 (CC BY 3.0).

Page 62 – Avon for Men print advertisement, source: eBay.com (PD image).*

Page 63 – Hertz Rent-a-Car 1962 print advertisement. Source: ebay.com. (PD image).*

Page 64 – Katherine Johnson, 1966. Photo by NASA, source: nasa.gov/image-feature/mathematician-katherine-johnson-at-work. (PD image). – *Hidden Figures* poster by 20th Century Fox, 2016.**

Page 65 – Depiction of Telstar 1, creator unknown. Source: en.wikipedia.org/wiki/Telstar_1. (PD image).
– Depiction of Mariner 2 by NASA/Jet Propulsion Laboratory. Source: en.wikipedia.org/wiki/Mariner_2. (PD image). – Albert Sabin, from *Its First Fifty Years*, by Theodore E. Woodward, M.D. of the U.S. Armed Forces Epidemiological Board. The photo is the work of a US Government employee and is in the Public Domain.

Page 66 – From *Newsweek* 19th Nov 1962.
Source: flickr.com/photos/91591049@N00/34867088672/. Attribution 4.0 International (CC BY 4.0).

Page 67 – Jackie Robinson by Osbrun. Source: en.wikipedia.org/wiki/Jackie_Robinson. Attribution-ShareAlike 4.0 International (CC BY-SA 4.0). – Jack Nicklaus, creator unknown. Source: commons.wikimedia.org/wiki/Category:Jack_Nicklaus. Attribution-ShareAlike 4.0 International (CC BY-SA 4.0).

Page 68 – Fonteyn and Nureyev at Schiphol airport, Amsterdam, by Eric Koch / Anefo. Source: commons.wikimedia.org/ wiki/Category:Rudolf_Nureyev. CC0 1.0 Universal (CC0 1.0) Public Domain Dedication.
– Seattle World's Fair, from *Life* Magazine 4th May 1962. Source: books.google.com.sg/books?id=3U4EAAAAMBAJ&printsec (PD image).* – Eichmann, 1942, photographer unknown.
Source: commons.wikimedia.org/wiki/Category:Adolf_Eichmann. (PD image).

Page 69 – Spider Man from *Amazing Fantasy* Issue #15, included here for information only under U.S. fair use laws. – Kennedys greet Bay of Pigs returnees, 28th Dec 1962. Source: en.wikipedia.org/wiki/Bay_of_Pigs_Invasion (PD image).

Page 70 – From *Life* Magazine 5th Oct 1962.
Source: books.google.com/books?id=eVUEAAAAMBAJ&printsec (PD image).*

Page 71 – From *Life* Magazine 12th Jan 1962.
Source: books.google.com/books?id=nU0EAAAAMBAJ&printsec (PD image).*

Page 72-74– All photos are, where possible, CC BY 2.0 or PD images made available by the creator for free use including commercial use. Where commercial use photos are unavailable, photos are included here for information only under U.S. fair use laws due to: 1- images are low resolution copies; 2- images do not devalue the ability of the copyright holders to profit from the original works in any way; 3- Images are too small to be used to make illegal copies for use in another book; 4- The images are relevant to the article created.

Page 75 – From *Life* Magazine 14th Sep 1962. Source: books.google.com/books?id=z00EAAAAMBAJ&printsec (PD image).*

Page 78 – Diet-Rite Cola print advertisement, source: eBay.com (PD image).*

Page 79 – Chesterfield King cigarettes print advertisement, source: eBay.com (PD image).*

*Advertisement (or image from an advertisement) is in the public domain because it was published in a collective work (such as a periodical issue) in the US between 1925 and 1977 and without a copyright notice specific to the advertisement.

**Posters for movies or events are either in the public domain (published in the US between 1925 and 1977 and without a copyright notice specific to the artwork) or owned by the production company, creator, or distributor of the movie or event. Posters, where not in the public domain, and screen stills from movies or TV shows, are reproduced here under USA Fair Use laws due to: 1- images are low resolution copies; 2- images do not devalue the ability of the copyright holders to profit from the original works in any way; 3- Images are too small to be used to make illegal copies for use in another book; 4- The images are relevant to the article created.

This book was written by Bernard Bradforsand-Tyler as part of *A Time Traveler's Guide* series of books.

All rights reserved. The author exerts the moral right to be identified as the author of the work.

No parts of this book may be reproduced, stored in any retrieval system, or transmitted in any form or by any means, without prior written permission from the author.

This is a work of nonfiction. No names have been changed, no events have been fabricated. The content of this book is provided as a source of information for the reader, however it is not meant as a substitute for direct expert opinion. Although the author has made every effort to ensure that the information in this book is correct at time of printing, and while this publication is designed to provide accurate information in regard to the subject matters covered, the author assumes no responsibility for errors, inaccuracies, omissions, or any other inconsistencies herein and hereby disclaims any liability to any party for any loss, damage, or disruption caused by errors or omissions.

All images contained herein are reproduced with the following permissions:
- Images included in the public domain.
- Images obtained under creative commons license.
- Images included under fair use terms.
- Images reproduced with owner's permission.

All image attributions and source credits are provided at the back of the book. All images are the property of their respective owners and are protected under international copyright laws.

First printed in 2022 in the USA (9781922676016).
Revised in 2024, 2nd Edition (ISBN 9781922676184).
Self-published by B. Bradforsand-Tyler.

www.ingramcontent.com/pod-product-compliance
Lightning Source LLC
Chambersburg PA
CBHW072104110526
44590CB00018B/3312